Creative Approaches to Elementary Curriculum

Creative Approaches to Elementary Curriculum

Margaret Merrion
Ball State University

Janet E. Rubin
Saginaw Valley State University

Heinemann
A division of Reed Elsevier Inc.
361 Hanover Street
Portsmouth, NH 03801-3912
Offices and agents throughout the world

The authors and publisher thank those who generously gave permission to reprint borrowed material:

"Asleep and Awake" from ONE AT A TIME by David McCord. Copyright © 1952, 1974 by David McCord. By permission of Little, Brown and Company.

Excerpt from *Lazy Jack and the Silent Princess* by Mitchell Motomora. Copyright © 1989. Reprinted by permission of the publisher, Raintree/Steck-Vaughn.

"Tooth Trouble" from TAKE SKY by David McCord. Copyright © 1961, 1962 by David McCord. By permission of Little, Brown and Company.

"Why Birds Are Never Hungry" from *Folk Stories of the Hmong* by Norma J. Livo and Dia Cha. Copyright © 1993. Reprinted by permission of the publisher, Libraries Unlimited, P.O. Box 6633, Englewood, CO 80155-6633.

"Some Love Coffee" and "The Farmyard" from ENGLISH FOLK SONGS FROM THE SOUTHERN APPALACHIANS, VOL. 1, edited by Maud Karpeles. © Oxford University Press 1932. Reprinted by permission of the publisher.

Library of Congress Cataloging-in-Publication Data

Merrion, Margaret Dee.
 Creative approaches to elementary curriculum / Margaret Merrion,
Janet Rubin.
   p. cm.
 Includes index.
 ISBN 0-435-08698-7
 1. Education, Primary—United States—Curricula. 2. Creative
activities and seat work. 3. Education, Primary—Activity programs—
United States. I. Rubin, Janet. II. Title.
LB1523.M47 1996
372. 19—dc20   96-45749
                 CIP

Editor: Lisa A. Barnett
Production: Melissa L. Inglis
Cover design: Barbara Whitehead
Text design: Saun L. Strobel
Manufacturing: Louise Richardson
Photo of Margaret Merrion by Ball State University Photographic Services
Photo of Janet E. Rubin by Portraits by Gregg

Printed in the United States of America on acid-free paper
99 98 97 96 DA 1 2 3 4 5 6 7 8 9

To Janet and Margaret
Partners in Creativity

Contents

Learning should be both a fundamental and fun part of a young child's school experience. For the teacher, this means building lessons upon creative choices which enliven curriculum. In this chapter, we examine conditions which challenge today's teachers of primary children. We make a case for employing teaching methods that bring about successful learning through creative and natural processes. We outline various learning styles, then jump right into an overview of creative music and drama activities. Guidelines are offered to assure successful implementation.

Chapter 1

ORIENTATION TO CREATIVE ACTIVITIES AND LEARNING STYLES

Factor #1

There's no question about it: a diverse group of children is coming to school and this diversity goes beyond ethnic, racial, and socioeconomic differences. The first few years—the most critical years of childhood development—are spent in strikingly different ways. Yet, in many of our nation's schools, we continue to classify and educate children in homogenous groups at certain grade levels. Teaching takes place, for the most part, in an intact group. (*Learning*, however, may not take place, for the most part, within an intact group.) Further, while each child arrives with diverse needs, abilities, interests, and cultural differences, the expectation remains for the classroom teacher to cover the core curriculum successfully with all children during the academic school year.

Factor #2

There's no question about another educational phenomenon: the core content today is broader and deeper than ever. Today's classroom teachers must address content that is relatively new to the curriculum. They have received mandates to include drug and sex education; computer competency; life management skills and career preparation; and global awareness, to name a few. Add to those new requirements the traditional (yet increasingly emphasized) content of science, mathematics, language arts, social studies, and physical education. The information age is exploding with new developments, many of which must find their way into elementary school curriculum, and the result is that the teacher is often in the dual roles of learner and mentor, assimilating new content in order to present the concepts to his or her pupils. This breakneck pace of expanding curriculum keeps teachers on their toes to keep abreast of the ever-inclusive and detailed content explosion. Some school districts have prudently allocated additional time for in-service, realizing the tremendous need to provide professional development for teachers. Still, teachers scramble to cover adequately the comprehensive content.

Factor #3

There's no question that teachers must seek innovative methods to help them teach effectively and efficiently, since time is limited. Although discussion and experimentation periodically grab our attention, the school year and school day, nationally, have not lengthened appreciably for decades. In fact, if any changes have occurred, they have truncated the amount of teacher-contact time with pupils. The need persists for better ways to teach—ways that can bring about effective and efficient learning.

While technology has much to promise, all admit it is no panacea to solving time, financial, or curricular pressures. Artificially intelligent computers, laser disks, hypermedia, and interactive technology have an undeniably valuable role in instruction. Technology, however, is not always current and, in some poorer districts, may not even be available. Regardless of other factors, there can be no substitution for the human communication of knowledge; much of the teaching/learning act remains between the intelligent and passionate teacher and the individual student. Further, even with the impressive advancements technology has offered to classrooms, we have yet to realize any teacher time saved.

Factor #4

Finally, there is no question that point of view has changed in terms of educational accountability. Today's teacher is expected to ask, "What have they learned?" not "What have I taught?" when evaluating the educational progress of students. The teacher is expected to instill in students the value of lifelong learning. Educators are being asked to respond to the demands of the workplace of the future and to provide training and experiences which will enable students to become adults who are able to compete productively in a global marketplace, respond with sensitivity to diverse populations, solve problems creatively, and work as team players. The once accepted notion that some would naturally fail in school is passé and the teacher is accountable to parents, accrediting agencies, administrators, and legislators, as well as numerous other interested bodies, for demonstrating progress with all children. The teacher will have both supporters and critics and must be prepared to answer to both.

Solving the Equation

Taking into account the factors of diversity, expanding curriculum, time limitations, and accountability, it is a challenge to solve this equation. We nonetheless forward one solution for your consideration: integrated learning through the arts. Specifically, we believe core content can be creatively combined in efficient and effective lessons using music and creative drama activities. It is a natural and logical solution to the enormous challenge facing today's educator.

We base this arts integration solution on certain premises:

(A) the arts are a natural and effective mode of learning for primary age children; and
(B) the processes used in arts activities can be vehicles through which other core content can be learned.

Our advocacy of the partnership of arts and core curriculum rests upon a solid foundation. For one thing, integrated learning through the arts occurs through a natural process. The content—be it mathematics, language arts, or science—is embedded with other disciplines. Because learning in life is not segmented into discrete thirty-minute lessons on one subject, integrated learning experiences parallel lifelong learning more realistically. As children grow and develop, their success with integrating content, creatively using knowledge to solve problems and generate ideas, and their ability to make connections will serve them well as contributing members of society. Learning, like life, does not happen in a vacuum.

Second, one of the most natural and effective ways to approach learning at the early childhood level is through familiar processes. The arts of music and creative drama are part and parcel of early childhood play. Children feel more secure in exploring new areas when their foray is grounded in the familiar. To employ such successful, natural, and enjoyable processes in an integrated manner for learning new content makes eminently good sense. Further, in using these arts to move from the familiar to the unfamiliar, children coincidentally build communication and social skills.

By approaching the curriculum creatively through the arts, children use an efficient method to acquire and retain knowledge and experience. The arts constitute a natural context in which children learn. Further, these processes accommodate diversities among learners. Music and creative drama lead them to new concepts and skills through various learning styles. With today's classroom being so complex, the more learning styles used, the greater the chance for reaching and meeting children's needs.

A Natural Learning Process

The beautiful thing about the arts and artistic expression is that they are natural. Observe any child who spontaneously bursts out in song, role-plays characters in skits, skips around the block with a sense of wonder and discovery, and makes castles and forts with sand, ice, mud, or any other natural resource available. Many children are "at home" with the artistic processes because they can freely express themselves through the art forms. The freedom and degree of comfort that accompany artistic play are integral aspects of the learning process. Clearly, the motivation, intrinsic inquiry, and fun inherent here are also conditions of successful learning.

But not all children have had the freedom and opportunity to grow and develop through the arts. A growing and alarming number of children have been placed before television sets, confined in playpens and cribs, and deprived of full sensory exploration. Such early, unnatural experience has an effect on the child's sense of inquiry and ability to grasp new knowledge from a nonvisual source. Active engagement in the arts serves to combat passivity and lack of sensory development.

An Accommodating Process

It is virtually impossible for an entire classroom of children to succeed if teachers do not recognize the different learning dispositions and learning styles children bring to school and if teachers do not cultivate methods of teaching which respect those contrasting preferences. Despite some bandwagon methods and materials that promise success, no single approach has been proven to be successful with all children in any subject area. The wise teacher seeks methods that develop *each* individual's potential. Since familiar methods (such as the learning processes in the arts) are especially effective in reaching unfamiliar content through varying channels of learning, a good case can be made for using the arts to teach the curriculum effectively.

It is amazing, then, that such a natural and valuable approach to learning is often side-stepped when children begin their formal education. Suddenly, the methods, the materials, and even some of the content are remote, isolated, and unnatural to the child's earlier stages of discovery. The appeal and positive results of conventional methods of classroom instruction (*e.g.*, large group lecturing, seat work, and significant visual/verbal work) sharply contrast among most children. The most well prepared (having enriched preschool experience) to the most at risk (having years of passive experience propped up before MTV) comprise typical classrooms.

Many aspects of formal schooling are restrictive. We often require children to sit still in their seats for long periods of time. We give many directions by word of mouth or through fine print at the head of a work sheet. We ask the children not to talk, hum, or sing. We ask them to think silently. We propose hypothetical and abstract scenarios or problems for them to solve. Notice something? It's a "we, we, we" classroom. It is teacher-centered. This type of learning environment is not child-centered. This formal experience is not attuned to the nature of a child. In this type of classroom, the prevailing point of view is, "What have I taught?" rather than, "What have they learned?" The question that should be guiding instructional practice is, *"What have we all learned?"* Without this question at the heart of instructional practice, it is no wonder children have difficulty acquiring and retaining information. To be sure, much of formal schooling does not accommodate the young learner at all.

Let's not forget another natural phenomenon: children are active learners. Using the arts to stimulate proactive learning is logical and productive. Because they are sensory-based, live, "now," and "me" activities that require children look, move, listen, touch, and manipulate, the arts draw children into engrossing experiences that naturally demand critical thinking. Arts-integrated lessons naturally beckon physical, mental, and sensory engagement, thus enveloping various modes of learning and accommodating the active nature of children. The arts are child-centered and work *with* the nature of the child, not against it.

Additionally, we have come to know that spontaneity, simultaneity, creativity, and divergence of play are important processes common to the arts that are transferable to thinking processes in core content. Unfortunately, as the child progresses through elementary school, many teachers ignore these obvious correlations. The musical and creative drama activities in this book forge and reinforce relationships with core curriculum. The activities approach core courses enterprisingly, effectively, and efficiently. And more importantly, by channeling this spontaneity, simultaneity, creativity, and divergence of student interests and abilities through arts activities, teachers open more doors. Students have greater opportunity to achieve academic gains in other core content areas.

At an Exploring New Dimensions conference in Detroit,[1] actor James Earl Jones noted that students enrolled in arts courses generally had higher academic scores than those not enrolled. Other speakers recognized the arts for their value as nonviolent means of self-expression and as vehicles for innovative thinking. To support their position, these speakers referred to the arts as ways of learning and urged our schools to look at arts not as enrichment but as a valuable and viable partnership of artistry and education. We support the belief that, if educators are to give more than lip service to their commitment to train our children for the workplaces of tomorrow, they should be expected to elevate arts education to a position of importance in terms of lesson planning and delivery. Here is a tool which taps the fundamental need to express oneself, communicate inventively, and spark creative fires. The arts ask students to be risk takers and to learn from their successes and their failures. These lessons have application going well beyond the original arts activity.

At present, some attention is also being given to the disciplinary and social values of the arts. These, too, strengthen the link to the curriculum. The student who increases attention span, becomes more academically motivated, learns to work with others, and channels negative energy into positive new directions through arts activity can, and often does, apply these benefits to other academic endeavors. The gains made through arts activities are by no means limited to those projects.

Learning Styles

Learning styles (or modalities) are the ways in which we perceive or "take in" information. In the learning process, each of us uses a set of take-up reels which give us multitrack readings of new experiences. Picture a toddler exploring a ball for the first time. The child touches it, tastes it, looks at it, shakes it, and perhaps even smells and listens to it. Each of these perceptions is recorded on the respective sensory reel and the concept of "ball" is formed. As the child encounters additional new concepts, these reels will be engaged repeatedly, however, certain reels may be favored. Sometimes, in fact, one sensory approach becomes dominant over another and fashions a clear learning style preference.

Learning style preference might be illustrated with a more complex task. For example, if children wish to learn a word processing program, they might elect to use one of the following styles:

---

[1]"Exploring New Dimensions: Business & Arts Partnerships Yield Higher Dividends," The International Center & Atheneum Hotel, Detroit, MI, October 29, 1993.

Visual (verbal): Some may approach the task by tackling a set of directions in a software manual. Or step-by-step directions could be understood in a tutorial which is presented on screen. The visual (verbal) learners "read all about it" and begin using the knowledge immediately at the computer.

Visual (nonverbal): Others may approach the task by observing another student word processing at the computer. They watch what commands are entered, how the mouse is operated, and what results are achieved. Then they attempt the same procedures as observed through their keen eyes.

Aural: These learners may be given a cassette tape (or instructions by lecture). As they listen to the directions, they execute the task. They depend on the oral word for guidance and internally "tape-record" the directions as a means of remembering.

Tactile/Kinesthetic: Yet others must manipulate the keyboard to acquire the skills. Like riding a bike, they cannot gain the skill by merely watching, reading, or hearing about it. This learning style depends on doing. The tactile feel actually is the best way in which kinesthetic learners remember the skill.

Most people can use each of the learning styles above. Depending upon the task—from following written directions in assembling a toy to understanding nonverbal and aural safety measures on an airplane—we need to develop all learning styles. Teachers have a responsibility for providing broad-based and comprehensive instructional methods which acknowledge and encourage multiple approaches to knowledge acquisition. The activities in this book encourage such development.

We know that children have clear preferences for how they want to learn. Younger children, for instance, learn better through visual (not necessarily verbal) than auditory experiences. But they learn best through tactile-kinesthetic experiences.[2] We acknowledge the importance of personal preference here but also advocate the need for children to develop all learning styles. Music and creative drama experiences refine auditory, visual, and tactile-kinesthetic learning styles, providing a distinct advantage in terms of multiplicity of approaches to comprehending and retaining content.

---

[2]Rita Dunn, "Modalities: An Open Letter to Walter Barbe, Michael Milone, and Raymond Swassing," *Educational Leadership*, February 1981: 381–382.

Another facet of learning concerns the modalities (the type or size of learning community) in which the child may excel.[3] Some children (especially gifted and talented) flourish in individual settings. Other children grow immensely in collaborative settings. Yet others may advance in partner or one-on-one dyads. Sensitivity to these factors can enhance the rate and degree of learning success.

The arts often involve fluctuations in the type and size of learning community. Certain experiences will require a collaborative process. Children will engage in experiences that build teams, involve give and take, foster constructive criticism, require cooperative groups, and draw on each child's strengths. Other times, the activities require private thinking and planning time or showcase an individual by placing attention solely upon his or her work. Some arts activities will be most fruitful if they involve duets or trios, as partner or small-group sharing will produce the best results. The learning communities are set naturally as children work alone or with others on projects.

The arts are especially effective in sharpening each learning style *and* engaging children in multiple learning styles. Today's teachers are expected to reach each child, regardless of learning ability, learning style, preferences/interests, and cultural differences. The arts not only recognize and accommodate such variances, but they celebrate and teach through the differences.

Finally, we would be remiss not to mention the obvious: the arts develop children's creative and expressive potential. Early childhood curriculum must address the place of music, creative drama, play, and movement in daily activities. We do a disservice to children if, by the time students get to the end of primary level, the arts are ignored unintentionally, as other core content consumes the school day. When we ignore the arts, we ignore our children. The arts are expressions of humanity and serve as expressive approaches to other content. Like the core of an apple, they can serve as a center both for the fruits of the curriculum and the child's curiosity. We hope that teachers will channel each child's expressive potential through the integrated arts activities contained in this book. Since every child has creative potential, each one is a "diamond in the rough," eager to be refined, to shine, and to contribute constructively and creatively as a citizen in our complex society.

You can see, then, why we advocate such processes beyond their obvious natural, efficient, and effective learning attributes.

---

[3]Rita Dunn and Nancy Reckinger, "Cultural Bias Model of Styles," *Educational Leadership*, November 1982: 75–76.

Approaching Core Content Creatively

We would like to introduce you to the repertory of music and creative drama activities that are used repeatedly throughout the chapters of this book. These activities range from simple ice-breakers which may last only a few minutes to fully developed lessons which may be the duration of a half hour or more. Each activity is presented through its definition (**what?**); its suggested participants (**who?**); the appropriateness and placement in the instructional setting (**where?**); its purpose (**why?**); and integration suggestions (**how?**).

Two terms are used throughout the text: replaying and sidecoaching. These describe practices designed to facilitate successful engagement in activities. We encourage their use.

Replaying simply means to repeat or do an activity again. There is no limit to the number of times an activity can be replayed. Several factors should guide this decision: (1) Does interest remain high? An activity should not be replayed to the point of boredom. (2) Will replay allow the incorporation of new ideas? (3) Will replay allow other or more children to become involved? Positive responses to numbers 2 and 3 are desirable. (4) Will replay provide an opportunity to refine skills or polish performance? The answer here should be affirmative. (5) Is replay a form of punishment? Replaying under the negative guise of "doing it until we get it right" should be avoided.

Sidecoaching describes comments and/or questions used by the teacher to deepen student involvement in an activity. The teacher's narrative should help the child to think or imagine more clearly. Questions such as, "How big is it?" "What color is yours?" and "It's really cold. How will these characters stay warm?" encourage creative responses. Statements such as, "You are making such special things!" "Your characters are working so hard," and "You all have made many good things to eat. We have salads and pies and breads to share" do so as well. Traditional forms of reply, however, should not be expected, as the teacher does not want children to speak or raise hands but rather to incorporate their ideas into their artistic interpretations. Sidecoaching can be done with the entire group or individually. In the latter situation, the teacher should simply speak quietly to the child who appears to have some difficulty getting into the activity. The same types of comments and questions are used whether sidecoaching in unison play or individually.

What?   **Name Games**

These are brief games which identify the children by name. Children may be challenged to categorize and/or remember facts and information. Name games invite them to participate as individuals as well as in group modalities. Generally warm-up or starter activities, these games often involve a name tag which may be related to the topic of study. Name games relax students socially while providing a point of focus to a lesson.

Who?   Primary grade level (K–3) children and the teacher. Every child has the opportunity to interact creatively and in a nonthreatening manner.

When?   Use name games at the beginning of the school year or to launch new lessons at any time. They are effective as "openers" and also useful in bringing divergent ideas together for closure.

Why?   To orient and familiarize children with one another; to introduce some new ideas; to motivate for additional exposure to content; to build individual confidence and group support; to foster divergent thinking; to strengthen visual learning style and aural learning style.

How?   Many names games reinforce visual learning through name tags, however, tags are not always necessary. Other games can reinforce an aural learning style by requiring children to remember what has been said previously. Introduce name games by always giving examples of typical responses. Be sure to allow sufficient thinking time to prepare responses and celebrate the wide variety of responses each child contributes. If a child seems unable to contribute an original idea but wishes to participate, allow repetition of ideas. If original thinking seems stymied, allow children to "pass" if they seem truly uncomfortable. As these often set the tone for other activities, use name games to foster a creative classroom climate.

What?   **Finger Plays/Chants/Nursery Rhymes**

This category of activities involves short poems or stories that typically have a rhythmic flow to them. They are recited en masse and often have finger, hand, or whole body movements that illustrate the action or respond to the beat of the lyrics.

Who?   Primary grade level (K–3) children and teacher.

When?   Use these activities to introduce a story or lesson related to content of the finger play, chant, or rhyme, as a short activity to vary pacing within a lesson, or as a prelude to more complex vocal or movement exercises.

Why?   To reinforce skills such as counting, rhyming, speaking clearly, and content related; to develop fine motor skills; and to develop tactile-kinesthetic learning style.

How?   It is wise to recite the finger play initially without movements to stress the words. Try to emphasize the beat when appropriate. Add motions and invite children to accompany you with the movements. Next, ask the children to recite the words with you. Finally, after enough rehearsal and repetition, allow the children to perform the finger play without your help.

What?   **Noisy Story**

Children are grouped by character in the story and recite a preassigned sound, word, phrase, or sentence each time that character is mentioned. Some stories also have unison characters to which all children respond. Responses should be spirited and on cue.

Who?   Primary grade level (K–3) children and the teacher.

When?   Integrate noisy stories at various points in the lesson; it is suggested that these be introduced when children are ready for simple stories.

Why?   To develop listening skills and the ability to respond on cue; to develop group skills; to cultivate vocal expression and speaking skills; to gain exposure to story structure and literary elements; to develop aural learning style.

How?   Write an original story or adapt a story from literature. Limit the number of characters and make sure that those characters appear regularly and in random order in the story. Add one unison character, if desired, for which the entire group responds. Also optional is a summary paragraph in which characters appear for a final time. Create a visual cue on the narrator's text to remind the reader to stop for sounds. Group the children by character and have each group practice the character's sound, word, phrase, or sentence before playing the entire story. When the children are confident of their character's sound, narrate the piece, having the children respond each time their character is mentioned.

What? **Pantomime**

Pantomime activities stress nonverbal communication. Children use their bodies rather than their voices to express thoughts, actions, and feelings.

Who?   Primary grade level (K–3) children; teacher participation in pantomime is optional as the teacher is often engaged in narrating the material.

When? Generally introduced after children have attained a level of comfort with basic beginning activities; integrated throughout lessons to underscore the importance of physical coordination and expression.

Why?   To be physically confident with oneself and to develop coordination skills; to apply observation and sensory awareness skills to clear physical communication of ideas, actions and emotions; to learn and practice fundamental movements; to use the body as a tool for characterization; to develop aural, visual (nonverbal), and tactile/kinesthetic learning styles.

How?   Pantomime activities involve physical responses to words, phrases, sentences, paragraphs, or stories. Children respond with their bodies upon hearing the material. Clarity, rather than complexity, of response is to be encouraged. In developing or selecting materials for pantomime, the teacher should look for those with inherent action or emotion as there must be something for the child to do or show. Use active verbs. If selected material contains a lot of descriptive passages, editing will be necessary.

It is recommended that the teacher start with simple pantomime activities and move to paragraphs and stories as children's skills develop. Orally sharing the material before play, replay, and sidecoaching are helpful techniques for leading pantomime activities.

What?   **Singing/Chanting**

The musical activities promote performance skills by developing in tune and/or rhythmical results.

Who?   Primary grade level (K–3) children and teacher.

When?   Integrate songs and chants at various points in the lesson, introducing a new idea; reinforcing or applying concepts; fostering divergent/creative thinking beyond concrete ideas.

Why?   To expand the voice as a natural avenue of expression; to develop one's singing or speaking voice tonally and rhythmically; to place important aural content (rhyming, items in succession, *etc.*) in units more easily grasped; to experience multicultural material; to develop aural learning style.

How?   First, sing the song to model the tune, words, and tempo for the children. Provide a starting pitch for the children to hum and match. Give them a signal to start, such as counting off or conducting. If the song is lengthy, have them repeat phrases or lines after you in echo fashion. At appropriate points, piece together sections to perform and repeat. Rehearse the melody, rhythm, and words enough so that the children can sing the song by themselves.

What? **Body Sounds**

Noises can be produced with the body such as stamping, toe-tapping, patting thighs (patschen), clapping hands, snapping fingers, or rubbing hands. The making of sounds is a precursor to performing instrumental sounds.

Who? Primary grade level (K–3) children with attention to progressive development of fine motor skills as youngsters mature.

When? Body sounds are appropriate to "stand alone" to form body sound orchestras (clapping, stamping feet, *etc.*); they may be used to accompany singing, chanting, or recorded music.

Why? To develop motor coordination; to lay foundation for instrumental work; to use the body expressively; to develop aural and tactile/kinesthetic learning styles.

How? Model the appropriate ways to execute movements, such as clapping hands by keeping one hand stationary while striking with the other. Practice body sounds together in different volumes and speeds. Allow children to select and vary body sounds for creative accompaniments. Be mindful that some students have not developed fine motor skills (such as snapping fingers) and provide alternate movements.

What? **Hand Jives**

These are clever arrangements or patterns of body sounds produced to the beat, such as clap, clap, snap, snap.

Who? Simple jives (grades K–1) to complex (grades 2–3) will vary according to motor dexterity.

When? Hand jives accompany chants, songs, or other events once the chant, song, or other material is well known.

Why? To develop motor coordination; to work in a solo, partner, or ensemble setting; to develop aural and tactile/kinesthetic learning styles.

How? Start with simple hand jives, such as a clap and patschen to a familiar song. Ask the children to keep the jive going while you sing. Then ask them to sing and perform the hand jive simultaneously. Encourage children to create new hand jives, making certain that the number of movements (usually 2, 3, or 4) fits the meter (time signature) of the song or chant.

When children have basic coordination skills mastered, have them perform hand jives with partners or in small groups.

What? **Playing Instrumental or Found Sounds**

Children can perform on classroom instruments such as drums, triangles, tambourines, rhythm sticks, maracas, cowbells, African thumb pianos, and sand blocks in a classroom "band." Or they can find noises to manipulate for special effects (jingling coins, tapping rulers on a trash can, *etc.*), using objects in their environment as sound sources.

Who? Primary grade level (K–3) children.

When? After children have had experiences chanting, moving, and using motor skills rhythmically, they are ready to extend the skills to instruments and objects.

Why? To expand repertory of sound potentials for expressive purposes; to sharpen attentive listening skills; to practice motor coordination and control; to practice ensemble playing; to develop tactile/kinesthetic learning style.

How? Introduce instruments one at a time, preferably one per day or week. Model the appropriate way to play the instrument. At a later date, invite children to explore different ways to find sounds on the instrument, always being respectful of the material.

Combine various groups of instruments for certain effects, such as all wooden sounds or all metal sounds. When children are able to perform in an ensemble, be certain to give them cues to start together, by counting off or conducting.

What?   **Creative Movement**

This activity involves moving to poetry, music, or other stimuli in a planned and sensitive way. Sometimes the movement involves the entire body; other times it may involve just arms.

Who?   Primary grade level (K–3) children.

When?   After children have learned basic fundamental movements and after they have had an opportunity to listen to the aural stimuli, they may engage in creative movement.

Why?   To use the body as an expressive tool; to develop tactile/kinesthetic learning style.

How?   We suggest a review of fundamental movements (marching, jumping, hopping, skipping, jogging, swaying, tiptoeing, kicking, reaching, stretching, pulling, pushing, *etc.*) prior to creative movement. Raise the children's awareness of many different ways and directions each of the simple movements can be varied. Always give children the opportunity to hear the poem, story, or music which is to be expressed through creative movement. Be mindful of the short attention spans and physical limits of young movers. Provide sufficient space.

What?   **Concentration Games**

Concentration games challenge mental acumen. Children contribute to concentration games by remembering and/or adding to series, stories, *etc.* These can be played in small or large groups.

Who?   Primary grade level (1–3) children with small groups and short series recommended for younger children and larger groups with more retention required as they become older and attention span increases.

When?   Integrate concentration games at various points in the lesson; introduce and focus upon lesson content; foster associative abilities.

Why?   To increase ability to pay attention, make associations, and retain information; to encourage quick and creative thinking; to build group support skills; to develop aural learning style.

How?   Any activity that relies upon attending to and applying content may fall into this category. The format may vary somewhat depending upon the game played. Two common designs are described below.

1. As a verbal activity, concentration games involve one person beginning a series and the next person repeating what that person has said before adding his or her own contribution. Following players must repeat what has come from others before adding their ideas.

2. As a nonverbal activity, players perform a series of actions and then repeat them as accurately as possible. For example, an exercise such as tossing a bean bag around a circle is played once. The actual object is then removed and the game repeated with the sequence being as accurately recreated as possible.

In either format as the game progresses, each person must successfully repeat what has gone before in order to add his or her own idea.

What?   **Circle Games**

The name refers more to the configuration in which the players are placed than to any one activity. Concentration games, group story building activities, and certain pantomimes are among the exercises commonly played as circle games.

Who?   Primary grade level (1–3) children, with simple games best for younger children and more complex games appropriate for older children.

When?   Integrate circle games at various points in the lesson; introduce and focus upon lesson content.

Why?   To increase concentration; to foster imaginative thinking; to build group support skills; to develop aural learning style and visual (nonverbal) learning style.

How?   Ask the children to sit or stand in a circle. Explain directions specific to the activity to be played.

What? **Quieting Activities**

These are designed to calm children and productively channel excess energy.

Who?   Primary grade level (K–3) children.

When?   At the end of a lesson or from within a lesson to direct its pace; quieting activities can also be used as transitions between lessons and/or activities.

Why?   To bring a sense of closure to an activity or lesson; to control pace within a lesson; to encourage correlation of physical and imaginative response; to develop visual (nonverbal) learning and aural learning styles.

How?   Playing quieting activities in pantomime is most effective. Children work with an image or descriptive sentence and then show their response. Allow adequate space and pace quieting activities appropriately. Suggesting that the children close their eyes before reacting frequently helps them to focus their responses without distraction.

What? **Listening Activities**

A directed task which draws children's attention to hearing subtleties of music or sound is a listening activity. The task is more than just hearing. It focuses attention on only what is heard and what it might express.

Who? Primary grade level (K–3) children.

When? For short periods of time, with specific listening tasks or activities which sustain attention, children can listen astutely. Keeping children engaged while listening (following charts, moving and so forth) will extend the duration of attentive listening.

Why? To develop aural learning style.

How? Select highly expressive music of brief (2–3 minutes) duration. Be clear in giving children specific listening questions or tasks to accomplish in order to keep the listening experience an active one.

What?   **Choral Reading**

Group recitation of literature (prose or poetry) with an expressive voice comprises choral reading. Interpretations may include unison, solo, and duo performances within a selection.

Who?   Primary grade level (2–3) children.

When?   Once children can read, memorize, and follow a conductor's directions, they are ready to perform choral readings.

Why?   To expand vocal expression; to work in ensemble setting; to develop aural learning style.

How?   Begin by reading the material and discussing its meaning. Ask the children to select words or phrases which are particularly expressive. "Word paint" by reciting special words or phrases to convey dramatic meaning. Determine how high, low, fast, slow, loud, or soft the selection should be. Designate a conductor or place the teacher in this role.

What? **Sound Journals**

This activity involves a place (usually a notebook) where children describe the characteristics of sounds; how the sounds make them feel; and what the sounds "look" like graphically. Sound journals record fine differences perceived aurally.

Who? Primary grade level (2–3) children.

When? Journals can be used any time children wish to describe and draw sounds, especially before music notation is taught. Journals are handy on field trips.

Why? To translate images from abstract to concrete form; to develop aural learning style; to develop visual (nonverbal) learning style.

How? The actual sound journal can consist of a number of pieces of writing and drawing paper stapled together. On one side, the child writes the name of the sound, when it was heard, and what it sounded like. The sound's meaning might be described, too. On the other side, the child should draw (color, paint, *etc.*) the sound. Verbal and nonverbal depictions of sounds can be compared individually or among groups.

What? **Group Story Building**

These activities constitute a form of story creation where more than one member of the class is responsible for the development of the plot and characters.

Who? Primary grade level (2–3) children.

When? Integrate group story creation at various points in the lesson after children have had some experience with concentration games and story structure; focus and assimilate content.

Why? To foster quick and creative thinking; to advance teamwork; to underscore dramatic and literary elements; to cultivate oral communication and listening skills; to develop visual (nonverbal) and visual (verbal) learning styles; and to develop aural learning style.

How? The most common approach to playing group story building as an oral activity is to ask the children to arrange themselves in a circle. The teacher begins a story. Each child then adds to the story, contributing as much as he or she desires.

Several parameters are popular within this category. Children might be limited to a single word or single sentence contribution; they might be asked to reverse fortunes, alternating positive and negative plot developments; they might be eliminated from the game if they repeat the previous player's last word or add "uh" or "um" as they pause to think.

Story starters might also be written. A variation here sees children selecting written topic sentences and basing their story upon the selection drawn. The parameters above may still come into play.

What? **Characterization**

Sometimes stand-alone exercises and sometimes a dimension of another activity, characterization emphasizes the physical and/or vocal creation of dramatic roles.

Who? Primary grade level (K–3) children, with simple characterizations expected of younger children and more complex and dimensional characterizations envisioned for older children.

When? Incorporate characterization activities when building upon observation, physical and/or vocal skills, working with prose or poetry, or focusing upon social interactions and feelings.

Why? To encourage honest portrayals; to generate empathy; to facilitate better understanding of self and others; to practice verbal and nonverbal communication skills; to develop visual (nonverbal) and visual (verbal) learning styles; and to develop aural learning style.

How? When emphasizing characterization, encourage clarity. As voice and body are primary tools for creating believable roles rather than caricatures, stress portrayals that clearly communicate what the character looks and/or sounds like. As children become more adept at creating characters, their interpretations should take on greater dimensionality.

What? **Improvisation**

These types of exercises are the spontaneous creation of music or dramatic work within a limited structure. Material is freely invented given minimal "kernels" of suggestion.

Who? Primary grade level (grade 3) children.

When? In music, improvisation is successful if children have a vocabulary of rhythmic and melodic patterns to use in their inventions. Creative drama improvisation is appropriate after children have attained a level of relative comfort and skill with pantomime activities.

Why? To cultivate divergent and creative thinking; to apply physical and vocal expressiveness to character development; to understand story structure and elements; to use as the basis for story creation; to generate a better understanding of characters and situations, or to test and explore ideas for dramatic interpretation; to develop visual (nonverbal) and visual (verbal) learning styles; and to develop aural learning style.

How? Improvisations in music might begin with completing a phrase to a chant, responding to a rhythmic pattern, or singing conversation creatively. Improvisations in creative drama can be done with dialogue or in pantomime. Dramatizations are rooted in the following structure:

> **Who**: (Who are the characters? The more description given, the more structured the characterizations should be expected to be.)
> **Where**: (What is the setting? Where does the action take place?)
> **What**: (What is the conflict or problem facing the characters?)
> **When**: (What is the time, day, month, season, *etc.*?)
> **How**: (How should the action be played?)

A dramatic improvisation might be based upon all five of the above or as few as two. Who and What are critical. Children should have only enough time to determine casting, use of dialogue, and setting. Discussing and planning plot development is not appropriate as this removes the activity from an improvisational format. If players are unable to bring an improvisational situation to a satisfying conclusion, the teacher might enter the play in role (as a character) and guide from within or else simply conclude the scenario.

What? **Role-Playing**

Role-playing combines characterization and problem solving by exploring difficult and multifaceted issues through dramatic play. The goal is not necessarily to solve the problem but rather to gain insight into points of view and available options.

Who? Primary grade level (grade 3) children.

When? Children should have some experience with improvisation, characterization, and story structure; integrate at various points throughout the lesson to analyze social and/or ethical choices and behaviors.

Why? To improve understanding of self and others; to generate empathic response; to cultivate divergent and creative thinking; to explore character relationships and experiences; to develop visual (nonverbal) and visual (verbal) learning styles; and to develop aural learning style.

How? Create and play these scenarios using the guidelines for improvisation. Role-playing situations should be problem centered and characters should have multiple options for response. After playing once, have the children switch roles and play the scenario again. After repeated play, lead a discussion with the children, exploring with them how they viewed the characters, how the characters might have felt, what else the characters might do in that situation, *etc*. At the conclusion of a role-playing scenario, students should have a better understanding of the problem and possible responses to it.

What? **Sequence Games**

This activity involves recognizing a cue and following with an assigned dramatic response. Successfully conveying, identifying, and ordering dramatic action are the paramount objectives of the game.

Who? Primary grade level (1–3) children; young children may need to see pictures rather than words on the cards.

When? Integrate sequence games at various points throughout a lesson to focus upon content and order.

Why? To reinforce concepts related to logical progression and form; to develop and strengthen visual (nonverbal) and visual (verbal) learning styles.

How? For sequence games, index cards and a master list are required. Index cards are randomly distributed to the children. The master list is for the teacher's benefit and is especially useful for recognizing action played out of turn. As the cards are not numbered, the master list charts the desired arrangement. If an error is made, consulting the list can confirm the problem and identify where the deviation occurred. Such an error, while not a desired outcome of the activity, can provide an opportunity to reinforce the importance of clarity in communication.

Prepare the index cards in advance. On one, write "You start the game. Come to the center of the room and (add the desired action)." On each of the other cards, write a cue and an action. Note the following example:

Cue: The person before you has pantomimed building a snowman.

You: Come to the center of the room and pantomime putting a hat and scarf on the snowman.

On each card, replicate the previous action as the cue, keeping the wording as exact as possible. It is helpful to write the cue in one color or font and the action in another to keep them distinct. When the children successfully recognize and play the actions, the result should be the dramatization of a logical story or sequence of events.

What?   **Story Creation**

Students orally, in writing, and/or through dramatization invent stories which can stand alone or be used later as material for story dramatization. Various stimuli, such as pictures and props, can serve as source material. Story creation can be done individually as well as in group modalities.

Who?   Primary grade level (1–3) children; young children are capable of simple creations although these activities are generally better suited to older children.

When?   Story creation serves as a precursor to story dramatization; some prior experience with or exposure to stories is helpful; integrate these activities at various points throughout the lesson.

Why?   To cultivate divergent and creative thinking; to strengthen communication skills; to gain understanding of literary and dramatic elements; to develop visual (nonverbal) and visual (verbal) learning styles; to develop aural learning style; and to develop tactile/kinesthetic learning style.

How?   Numerous activities fall within this category. Several are described below.

Story Creation from Improvisation: Using the improvisational format described previously, replay scenarios, fleshing them out each time and, if desired, adding scenes until a complete story has been developed.

Story Creation from Pictures: Play with individual children or with children arranged in small groups. Give each group a photograph, reproduction, or picture. Have the children create a story based upon the picture.

Story Creation from Props: Play as you would with pictures, using one or more props to create the story. Props can be used as they are in reality or the condition can be added that a new use be found for them in the story. Stories can incorporate one or several props.

Open-ended Stories: Children are given the beginning of a story and they must add to and complete it. When using this format, it is best to limit the number of contributors to five and to be certain that beginnings lend themselves to multiple avenues of plot development. Open-ended story starters can stop anywhere, even mid-sentence, so long as multiple opportunities for plot development result.

What?   **Story Dramatization**

Using original poetry or prose or material from published sources, children bring all of their previously practiced dramatic skills to bear in story dramatization. Here, the emphasis is upon bringing the material to life through development of character and plot, communication of dramatic action, use of dialogue, understanding of theme, relating to setting and spectacle, and assimilation of dramatic techniques and skill development.

Who?   Primary grade level (K–3) children. Young children should be given very simple poems and stories with which to work while older children should be challenged with more complex material.

When?   Story dramatization should be incorporated at various points throughout a lesson or should stand as a solo activity. These are recommended for children who have had exposure to creative drama and have some level of skill development. They should be a part of the lesson only when there is adequate time to work on the material, as these rarely yield in-depth portrayals when played quickly or without replay. Use these to focus upon lesson content.

Why?   To refine previously acquired skills; to expand empathic response; to improve vocal and physical expressiveness; to foster creative thinking; to better understand self and others; to engage in teamwork; to improve understanding of content including literary and dramatic elements; to develop visual (verbal), visual (nonverbal), aural, and tactile/kinesthetic learning styles.

How?   Share the material to be dramatized with the children and be certain that they comprehend it. You may, for example, wish to read a story several times before playing it. Ask questions and discuss the material with the children. Have them identify the scenes and the important action that must occur within each. Select the scenes to be developed through dramatic play and do not feel obligated to do an entire story if the students are interested only in certain portions.

Now, focus upon the first scene to be played. Who are the major characters in that scene? Children should individually "try on" each of those characters. This is done by first having the children close their eyes and imagine the character. Ask each child for a brief description of what he or she sees to be sure that the child has an idea to play. Children then show, in pantomime, the character as they envision him or her engaged in some sort of action. This action can be something mentioned in the story or something that just seems logical for that character to do. Play this "try on" in unison and in pantomime. Repeat this kind of "try on" for each major character in the scene.

Following this, ask the children for suggestions as to what the characters might say in the scene. Place the children in pairs or small groups and determine a part of the scene to play, having each child assume one of the characters in that part. Dialogue is used here. All of the groups play at the same time and the teacher would do well to check on each as they work through the action. The teacher then asks for or calls upon students to play the part they have just worked on for the entire class.

Assessment follows with attention directed first at what has worked well and next upon what can be improved. If possible, direct critical comments to the character rather than the student. Opportunity to replay should follow. This pattern of assessment/replay should be ongoing until the children are satisfied with the work. The rest of the scene should be approached in the same manner and the technique is then repeated for each scene in the story. Individual scenes can be linked as each is successfully developed or at the completion of play. Regardless of the choice here, when scenes are reconstructed, the result should be an in-depth and lively interpretation of the story.

Using This Book

The experiences which follow are designed to integrate core content for elementary curriculum (K–3). By core content, we mean the subject areas that are common to the elementary curriculum:

Arts education
Health
Language arts (reading, writing, speaking, and listening)
Mathematics
Multicultural education
Physical education
Science
Social studies
Technology

By examining curriculum guides used in various states across the nation, basic skills and concepts were extracted for representative activities. This content is not exhaustive nor all inclusive. Rather, it represents common units of instruction that serve as examples for arts integration. Teachers may extrapolate the activities to slightly different content easily, once the creative process is understood.

Chapters are organized according to the content areas. Each chapter begins with an overview chart to serve as an advance organizer for the material to follow. The chart contains two columns. The content column lists representative concepts or skills. The music/creative drama column juxtaposes the arts activities used to teach the content. When first starting some of the activities, it will be useful to refer back to this chapter to review suggestions for implementing the lesson.

Each activity has a recommended grade-level icon. While our experiences have placed the activities in these suggested maturity levels, we trust that teachers will accommodate the activity to the skill and ability levels of their children.

We have a few general recommendations for guiding the creative process and managing the classroom. Many teachers are concerned about classroom control during creative experiences. While it is true that the instructional benefit is lost if children are out of control, a special type of environment that fosters creativity without chaos or military regime is optimal—and possible!

In establishing a classroom environment conducive to creative participation and risk taking, it is important to let the children know that *you* value these kinds of experiences. Let the children know that the arts are an equal partner in an integrated lesson and not simply a means to an end to more important subject matter. Participate with students on whatever level you are comfortable, whether that be as narrator of a story, member of the found sound orchestra, or character in a story dramatization. Praise when the children's effort merits it, set high standards for achievement, let the children know that it is alright to fail if a creative risk has been undertaken sincerely and be supportive and interested.

Certain practices will also serve you well. Ask open-ended questions whenever possible as you guide activities that will challenge thinking and stimulate the imagination. Expect less structured responses than might be typical in more traditional instruction but be certain that the children know that this type of activity does not mean that anything goes; limits are still appropriate and behaviors that limit the enjoyment or benefit of the activities for the child or classmates are unacceptable. It is sometimes useful to ask for "preview play," which is an advance look at what children intend to do.

If you must discipline a child, let him or her know that it is behavior to which you are responding and not personality. If, after having exhausted other methods of curtailing inappropriate behavior you must ask the child to leave the activity, also invite him or her to rejoin when ready to contribute positively. Should a child not wish to play an activity or be unable to think of a contribution, don't put the child on the spot. Make every effort to send a positive message to the children about the value of these experiences.

In planning lessons, think about effective links to other content areas and let objectives and outcomes guide your choice of activities. Also, give some consideration to how you will motivate at the start of a lesson, transit between activities, and bring the lesson to closure. Weigh time factor and ability level of the participants and match activities accordingly. Asking a child to be creative and following that instruction with a charge to rush is often contradictory. Anticipate questions the children will ask when developing directions. Being child-centered and focusing upon student learning, rather than being teacher-centered and focusing upon your efforts, will bring better results.

Chapter 2

ARTS EDUCATION

Content	Music/Creative Drama	
Art: Production Skills	Finger Play:	Art is Fun
	Pantomime:	My Art Supplies
		Look Closely
	Story Creation:	Mural
Shape Recognition	Body Sculptures:	Making Shapes
Color Recognition	Noisy Story:	Michelangelo van Gogo's Paints
	Pantomime:	Primary and Secondary Colors
	Story Dramatization:	Pastel Park
Music Reading	Name Game:	Fascinating Rhythm Names
		Musical Notation Names
	Chant:	Chants for You and Me
		Peas Porridge Hot
		Orchestra Call
		The Muffin Man
Instrument Identification	Name Game:	Instruments
		Instrument Names
	Noisy Story:	Frieda the Flute
	Pantomime:	Instrument Characterization
Experiencing Meter	Hand Jives:	When the Saints Go Marching In
		Take Me Out to the Ball Game
	Accompaniment:	ABA Triple Meter
Melody	Listening:	Melodic Puppets
Rhythm	Body Sounds:	Beat in the Feet/Band in the Hand
		Rhythmic Dialogues
Aural Skills	Musical Questions and Answers:	Warm-up
		For Your Ears Only
Chanting	Chant:	Miss Mary Mack

continued

Content	Music/Creative Drama	
Timbre	Scavenger Hunt: Found Sound:	Scavenger on Assignment Band from Scratch
Improvisation	Improvisation:	Punchinella Improvising for Grids Creative Conversations Improvisation Cards
Creative Interpretation and Conducting	Creative Movement:	The Listener as Conductor
Style	Listening:	What's the Same? What's Different? Musical Style Show
Music Literature	Listening and Moving: Listening:	Music Connections Name That Tune

rts education includes music, creative drama, and the visual arts. The activities in this chapter are designed to bring about increased understanding and enjoyment of these art forms. Each activity can stand alone or serve as part of a sequence of exercises to bring about comprehension of and experience in arts content.

Art Is Fun

(Finger Play)

The children will derive double enjoyment from the following activities as they explore art production skills through creative drama. This finger play serves as a simple warm-up to start the children thinking about art. Recited in unison, it helps young children to recognize as *art activities* things they may think of only as fun or *play*. This beginning activity helps children to make the important connection between art production and enjoyment.

Paint a picture.	(Make a dabbing motion.)
Draw with crayons.	(Move hand as if drawing.)
Form a ball with clay.	(Mold imaginary ball.)
Cut the paper.	(Move fingers as if using scissors.)
Brush the paste.	(Brush back and forth.)
Let's do this all day!	(Smile!)

My Art Supplies

(Pantomime)

Gr. 1-2

This poem serves as a tool for discussing proper care of art supplies. Following a class art activity, children can incorporate this pantomime into the clean-up process as they tidy their work areas.

"Clean up this mess," my Mother said,
"Or you'll be sent straight off to bed."

She walked away. Now, here I stand
Holding my scissors in my hand.

I fume. I fuss. This isn't fair.
My crayons are scattered everywhere.

My purple crayon's crushed on the floor.
I step on it; it is no more.

I gather up the rest with haste.
Oops! I spill a jar of paste.

I rinse my paintbrush in the sink.
The bristles aren't so stiff, I think.

Pick up my drawings. Make a stack
Of paper. Put scraps in a sack.

Now one last thing — a ball of clay.
There! I put them all away!

Advancing Skill:

★ With the children, determine what other art supplies might be used. Invite the children to pantomime the character in the poem putting these away.

Upon completing the poem and the advancing skill above, you and the children can make a list of all the art supplies shown in their pantomimes. Along with art materials, describe their proper care. It is fun to use crayons, paints, or colored chalk for this list and to display it in the classroom, creating a visual reminder of materials and care.

ART SUPPLY	PROPER CARE

Children also enjoy showing what happens when art supplies are not given proper care. Afford opportunities for them to pantomime painting with stiff brushes, show how they would look if they were stiff brushes caked with dried paint, and demonstrate similar results of neglect with other art materials.

The previous two activities treat basic concepts for young learners. These next two activities challenge older children to study art with their eyes and ears.

Look Closely
(Pantomime)

Older children can be introduced to art history and gain insight into art criticism through this activity. By studying famous paintings, reproductions, or prints, children sharpen critical observation skills while analyzing artistic process and intent.

As an introduction to critical observation, have the children study prints of famous paintings and identify people or objects in each print that can be interpreted through pantomime. Several prints (or similar materials) should be selected for study and children given ample time to view each. Prompt thinking with questions such as, "What was the artist trying to say in this work?" "What does the artist want you to think or feel when you see this?" and "What do you think is the most important image in this picture?" The class can then generate a list of people or objects in the prints that appear significant to them. After an appropriate list has been developed, call out the subjects and ask the children to pantomime them.

Examples:

> a dog walking
> a woman pushing a baby carriage
> a bird flying
> a woman smiling
> a man rowing a boat

Sidecoaching questions and statements such as, "Why are you smiling?" "How quickly or slowly are you walking, little dog?" and "Some of you are working up quite a sweat as you row" deepen involvement and identification with the work.

Upon completing the pantomimes, encourage children to share their thoughts and reactions. How did they feel about a character? Who was the person? Why did the artist capture him or her in that particular way? Use these probing questions when evaluating the activity to verify that children are looking beyond the surface of the work for artistic relevance. We have delighted, for example, in a child's recognition that a portrait painter was like a photographer before cameras were invented!

Advancing Skill:

★ The children may want to combine some of these characters and use them in a story creation, incorporating a setting from one of the prints. Dialogue can be added at this time.

Mural

(Story Creation)

Just as children **Look Closely** in the previous exercise, **Mural** invites them to *listen closely*. Music suggests pictures to the imagination and this activity invites children to put those pictures into concrete form.

While teachers frequently provide background music during art activities, rarely do children have the chance to demonstrate their musical imaginations in a complete and satisfying way.

Rather than treating the music as "wallpaper music," *i.e.*, present but not really a point of focus, this mural activity invites children to give shape to their thoughts and feelings associated with a piece of music. Whether they have visions of sugar plums or rap jive movements dancing in their heads, the teacher's task is to guide the children to develop their imagery into a visual story told through a mural.

Begin with musical literature that is programmatic and concrete such as *Peter and the Wolf*. After discussing major episodes, assign children to particular scenes of the story to work on panels of the mural. Let the children flesh out details of the story through visual elements (colors, shape, perspective, and line). Draw their attention to musical aspects which help tell the story (volume, speed, instrumentation).

Next, children can progress to more abstract listening exercises connected to various content areas. The class, for example, could be divided into groups with each group painting a picture based upon *Pinocchio*, *Pocahontas*, *Sleeping Beauty Ballet,* or *The Nutcracker Suite* (language arts) or using other pieces of music such as *La Mer* (science); *The Blue Danube* or *The Moldau* (social studies). The children create the mural prior to learning the title and/or story of the music.

This exercise encourages active listening. Ask the children what story they hear in the music. Do they all hear similar stories? How does the story they have envisioned match the actual title of the piece? What do they think the composer had in mind? These are only some of the questions that can be used to help children compare/contrast while integrating concepts from several content areas.

We enjoy our students' reactions when we reveal the title of a piece *after* they have completed their murals. This invites discussion about what they heard in the music that suggested images to them, what the composer wanted them to hear, and how knowing the title influences their perceptions of the piece.

Making Shapes
(Body Sculptures)

In *Look Closely* and *Mural*, children may recognize how shapes are used to create art work. *Making Shapes* gives them an opportunity to create forms with their bodies. They can convert themselves into the geometric figures used by visual artists.

To play, the teacher selects the number of children needed to make each shape, whispers the shape to them and gives them some rehearsal time. Children use their bodies to create the shapes. Six children, for example, would be used to form a rectangle. They could do so by lying on the floor and connecting limbs so that four form the top and bottom and two form the sides. Larger versions of the shapes can be created by using more children to form each sculpture.

Other suggested shapes are circle, triangle, and square. We recommend that all shapes be assigned and that children rehearse simultaneously. Groups then show their body shape sculpture to the rest of the class and viewers identify the shape they see.

Advancing Skills:

★ A large space is suggested for this advancing skill. Divide the class into two groups. Each group should prepare a body sculpture in which several shapes are linked. One, for example, might have a triangle, a circle, and a square linked by connecting body parts. The other group has to identify the shapes present in the sculpture.

★ Invite the children to invent new shapes and demonstrate them for the larger group. Together, assign creative titles to their original inventions.

Michelangelo Van Gogo's Paints

(Noisy Story)

Gr.
1-2

Young children can gain experience with color recognition when playing this noisy story.

Children should form six groups. Each group is assigned a color and the color's response "rehearsed" before playing begins. The Red Paint group, for example, responds with "I'm important" every time Red Paint is mentioned in the story. We suggest asking all students to play Mr. Nelson and Michelangelo van Gogo in unison and to play the colors as individual group sounds. After the children have practiced their assigned sounds, play the story.

Mr. Nelson — He's coming!
Michelangelo van Gogo — I'm a famous artist
Yellow Paint — I'm bright
Green Paint — Pick me, please
Orange — I'm a fruit color

Red Paint — I'm important

Blue Paint — I'm pretty
Violet — I'm delicate

"He's coming! He's coming here to my store!" Mr. Nelson*, the shopkeeper, was so excited as he hung up the phone. "I must tell my wife that the famous artist, Michelangelo van Gogo*, is coming to my art supply store to buy new paints!" Mr. Nelson* ran out of the store. Mr. Nelson* could be heard yelling, "He's coming," as he ran down the street.

When the store was empty, the paints began to talk to each other. "He'll pick me," said Red Paint*. "He'll pick me," said Yellow Paint*. "He'll pick me," said Blue Paint*. "We're primary colors," said Red Paint*, Yellow Paint*, and Blue Paint* in unison. "He needs us to make other colors," said Red Paint*.

Farther down the display case, with his friends Violet* and Orange*, sat Green Paint*. "I wish he'd pick me," Green Paint* said softly. Red Paint*, Blue Paint*, and Yellow Paint* heard Green Paint* and started to laugh. "You!" snickered Yellow Paint*. "Why would he pick you? Green Paint* can't make the sun in a painting shine like I can." Blue Paint* also teased Green Paint*. "You! Green Paint* can't make a sky in a painting. Only I, Blue Paint*, can do that." Red Paint* sneered at Green Paint*. "I am a primary color. Blue Paint* is a primary color. Yellow Paint* is a primary color. We're important. You, Green Paint*, are a secondary color. You are not as important as we are." "That's not true. Don't listen to them," said Violet* and Orange* as they tried to comfort Green Paint*. "We are just as important as they are."

Just then the door to the shop opened and Mr. Nelson* walked in with Michelangelo van Gogo*. Michelangelo van Gogo* walked to the display case where the paints sat proudly. The artist looked at all of the colors. "That one," said Michelangelo van Gogo*, pointing to Green Paint*. "I want that one. I want grass in my next painting and this is the perfect shade of green for grass." With that, Michelangelo van Gogo* lifted Green Paint* from the display case, paid for him, and left the store.

Red Paint*, Blue Paint*, and Yellow Paint* were speechless. "Green Paint* is going to become famous," said Violet*. "Yes," said Orange*, "Michelangelo van Gogo's* paintings hang in museums all over the world. Many people will get to see Green Paint* now."

And it was true. Green Paint* made the green grass in Michelangelo van Gogo's* new painting and became famous.

Advancing Skills:

★ Using watercolors, each child makes three pictures. The first uses only the primary colors in this story, the next the secondary colors, and the third all six colors. All of these pictures are then used to make a *My Class Big Book* that is divided into three sections: (1) Primary Colors; (2) Secondary Colors; and (3) Primary and Secondary Colors.

★ Write and play a new noisy story that uses primary and secondary colors as characters.

Primary and Secondary Colors

(Pantomime)

Second and third graders can work on color recognition and affective response to color through pantomime sentences. Ask the children to perform the following actions and then tell how each of the colors made them feel.

You are the bright yellow sun shining in the summer sky.

You are a blue wave crashing against the shore.

You are an orange squirting your juice into a pitcher.

You are a blue bird flying across the blue sky.

You are a violet opening your petals.

You are a red cardinal building your nest.

You are an orange flame flickering atop a candle.

You are a yellow jacket buzzing around a flower.

You are a green leaf floating gently to the ground.

You are a green bug crawling along the ground.

You are a red fire engine speeding to the scene of a fire.

You are an African violet growing in a pot.

Advancing Skill:

★ Children will enjoy creating and playing their own pantomime sentences that incorporate primary and secondary colors. At the close of the activity, invite the children to tell how the colors in these new sentences made them feel.

Pastel Park

(Story Dramatization)

With *Primary and Secondary Colors*, children start associating color and feeling. The following story strengthens this connection by encouraging them to explore the relationship between colors and feelings. The story dramatization format fosters an empathic response to each main character.

"This is going to be really weird," Amber said to her friend, Violet, as they got off the bright yellow school bus. "I hope we don't feel out of place," Violet replied.

The third grade class at the Rainbow Elementary School had been promised a special field trip as an end of the school year treat. Today, all of the children in Ms. Shade's class had been driven to Pastel Park for a picnic.

"Everything here is very soft," said Ms. Shade to the children as they stepped off the bus. "You may explore, but come back here in an hour for lunch."

"Let's go," said Amber and she and Violet raced down a hill covered with pale yellow buttercups. "Look," Violet exclaimed, "a lake."

The two girls ran to the edge of the clear, pale water. Amber saw a fragile soft gray shell floating on the surface. She fetched it from the water. Suddenly, a strange creature popped up from beneath the surface. "Welcome to Aquamarine Lake," it whispered. "Don't be frightened. Everyone talks softly in Pastel Park. You have picked the enchanted shell from the water and that's my signal to give you a tour of the park. Look into the water. You'll see coral and pale green sea sprites. You must, however, leave before the tide comes in because the tidal foam green waves are much darker." With that, the creature laughed and then disappeared. The friends looked at each other in amazement. "Did we really see that?" asked Amber. "What was it?" wondered Violet.

The girls climbed up a big hill and found themselves in a lovely garden. "Do you like the lilac trees?" The strange creature appeared again. "I'm particularly fond of these pink roses. Come over here." In a flash, it was standing by a large bush. "Smell these buds. Lavender. So lovely." The girls walked to the bush, bent over to smell the tiny buds, and when they looked up the strange creature was gone.

"I can't believe what I'm seeing," said Violet. "I think it's fun," said Amber, always the more daring of the two. "There's a sandy area over there," she said, pointing to a distant spot. "Let's have a look."

Amber and Violet arrived at the sandy dune only to find the creature waiting. "What took you so long?" he chided. "I love this spot in the summer. You can stretch out on the beige sand, watch the white clouds roll by in the clear blue sky, and get a tan. I like to bring a soft pillow and a silver blanket in case I fall asleep. Well, I must go now. I hope you enjoyed the tour."

"Wait," both girls shouted. "Shhh. Speak softly," the creature said. Violet blushed. "Please tell us who you are," implored Amber.

The creature looked serious. "Who I am is not nearly so important as why I am. There are so many harsh colors in the world. Remember to see that which is soft and gentle and to look with your heart as well as with your eyes." With that, he was gone.

The girls stood silently. Violet finally said in a hushed voice, "They'll miss us at lunch. Let's go back."

When they arrived at the picnic site, Ms. Shade greeted them. "Did you girls make any interesting discoveries?" she asked. Amber and Violet looked at each other and smiled.

Advancing Skill:

★Children can create their own stories about adventures that might take place in *Pastel Park*. They can then select several of these to dramatize. In evaluation, the teacher can prompt them to talk about what affective associations to color are found in these new adventures.

Fascinating Rhythm Names
(Name Game)

Part of the creative act involves manipulation of sounds, movements, and actions. Children are natural inventors, and they need a set of symbols to organize and manipulate. The symbols used for rhythmic notation provide the opportunity to understand and create rhythms simply.

We begin with the most personal and important of speech patterns: the children's names. Make name tags large enough to write the children's names and the rhythm of their names. For example:

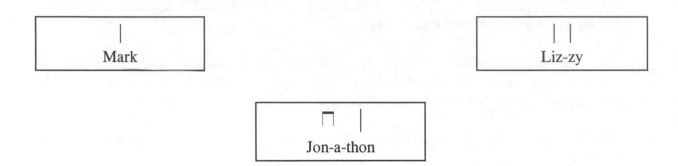

Activities should help children learn one another's names and read the rhythm of the name from the name card.

1. Have children stand in a circle and say their names rhythmically.

2. On the second time around, children then repeat their names while clapping the rhythm.

3. When every child can say and clap his or her name correctly, the group repeats each child's name.

4. For the final round, let the hands do the talking, *i.e.*, the group claps the rhythm of each child's name without voicing it.

Musical Notation Names

(Name Game)

After *Fascinating Rhythm Names*, children will be confident to go beyond the rhythms of first names. For this activity you will need to give the children a piece of tag board (approximately 4 inches by 9 inches). They will also need a piece of yarn about two feet in length and a hole punch. The yarn will be attached to the top two corners so that the children can wear their name tags. See the following illustration.

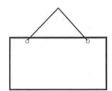

Ask the children to notate their full names and rhythmic notation on the card. If possible, each name should fill the length of four beats. Use rests to complete the measure if necessary. For example:

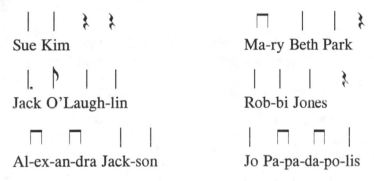

Sue Kim

Ma-ry Beth Park

Jack O'Laugh-lin

Rob-bi Jones

Al-ex-an-dra Jack-son

Jo Pa-pa-da-po-lis

Full notation names on cards become the basis for several clever re-combinations for short rhythm pieces. Help the children view each card as one rhythm pattern. Each pattern can be juxtaposed for different effects. Encourage the children to discover these differences through the following exercise.

In groups of six, let the children clap their names from the notation cards and "string" them together into a six–card phrase. Ask them to experiment by re-ordering the rhythm in various combinations until they like the outcome. For example, when the six names are strung together, the children might discover that the rhythm patterns seem to get "busier" and more complicated. Reversing them, as in the following version, might create an entirely different effect.

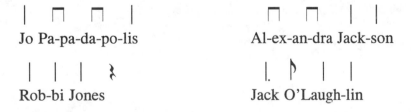

Jo Pa-pa-da-po-lis

Al-ex-an-dra Jack-son

Rob-bi Jones

Jack O'Laugh-lin

Ma-ry Beth Park   Sue Kim

Other versions will create even further differences. Finally, extend the creative exercise and give each group a set of rhythm instruments to perform their best rhythm for the class.

Chants for You and Me
(Chant)

Another way to gain familiarity with each other's names is through the next chant. Have the children sit in a large circle. Keep the beat by establishing a patschen (patting thighs) pattern which alternates left and right hands. Learn the group chant:

Group:	We're starting together A game of our names. When your turn arrives, Announce your name. The beat starts here.
First child:	My neighbor is . . .
Second child:	Alice.
Group:	Alice.
Alice:	My neighbor is . . .
Tony:	Tony.
Group:	Tony.

The activity continues until every child has a chance to say his or her name without losing the beat. Close the introductions with the group chant, changing the final line to, "The beat ends here!"

Peas Porridge Hot

(Chant)

This rhythmic reading activity starts with a familiar chant having recognizable patterns, but it moves to an unfamiliar one and encourages creative experimentation.

Speak the chant with a decided emphasis on the rhythm:

Peas porridge hot.   Some like it hot.
Peas porridge cold.   Some like it cold.
Peas porridge in the pot   Some like it in the pot
Nine days old.   Nine days old.

Advancing Skills:

★ Teach the children the rhythmic syllables to the chant:

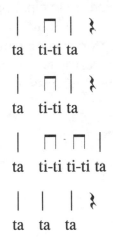

★ To feel the rests that occur within the chant, clap on the rhythms and open hands on the rest beats.

★ Place the rhythmic notation of the lines on individual cards. Perform the rhythm in order. Change the order of the cards and perform it accordingly. For example, a new configuration might look as follows:

★ Pass a bean bag to the beat (including the rests) while reciting the chant.

Orchestra Call

(Chant)

There are lots of different instruments about which children might be curious. They are likely to have familiarity with many types of guitars, saxophones, drums, and other MTV instrumental ensembles. What about some of the other instruments in a marching band, municipal band, or symphony orchestra? These instruments form a foundation of knowledge which little ones can enjoy as they contemplate possible study of traditional instruments for school bands and orchestras. One way to learn more about the instruments of the orchestra is to chant the information in the following call. Encourage the children to emphasize the rhythm as they recite:

Orchestra Call

Pic-co-lo pic-co-lo   pic-co-lo pic-co-lo   I'm the high-est

to be found!   Flutes are clear and   bright in sound.

O-boe and Eng-lish horn   dou-ble reed twins   look a-like, sound a-like,

cou-sin wood-winds!   Clar - i - net, you can bet,   prac-tice the sound ba-

soon drops . down be-   low the ground.

What is so French a-   bout the horn?   Trum-pets and trom-bones

sound less for- lorn than the tu- ba, tu- ba   bet-ter not prac-tice in ear-ly morn!

Tim-pan-i are | ket-tle drums that | can be

tuned. Then there's | chimes and bells and | oth-er good drums like the

snare, bass, | tom- tom and bong-o | all in the fa - mi - ly

of per | cus- sion!

Fi - nal - ly we get to | strings of the or- ches- tra | heart of the or- ches- tra

Vi - o - lin sweet-ly | sing-ing up high. Vi- | ol - a is lar -ger and

plays a bit low-er. | You must sit down to | play the cel - lo but

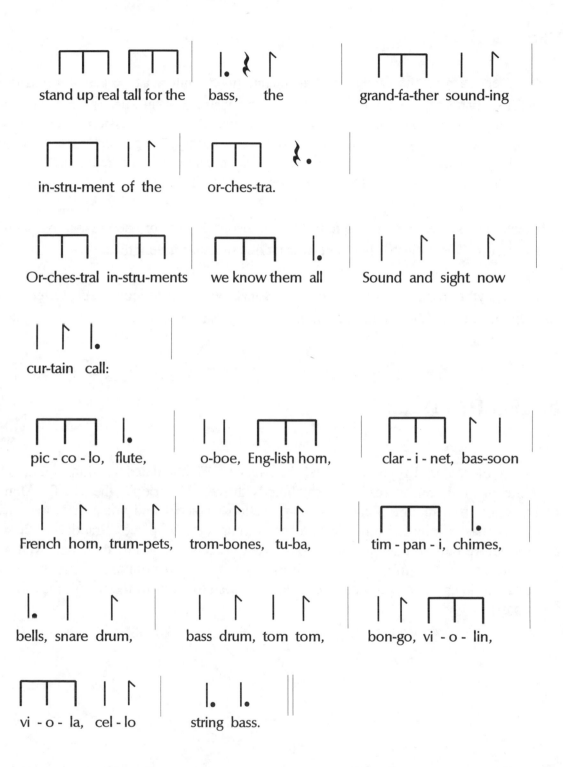

Advancing Skills:

★ After learning the *Orchestra Call* chant, invite children to create ostinati (a short repetitious pattern) based upon the sounds of the instrument families (such as bowing and plucking) or the names of the families (woodwind, brass, percussion, and string). For example, one ostinato might be "toot, toot," or "buzz-y, bang," or "rat-a-tom ching," voiced by a small group. The ostinato pattern serves as an undercurrent of softer but persistent sounds to accompany the children chanting the call.

★ Ask the children to compose four different ostinati—one for each respective family of instruments. The ostinato should be at least one measure in length.

★ The rhythm of the chants and creative ostinati will suggest movement. Offer children the opportunity to choreograph movements to express the action!

The Muffin Man
(Chant)

Can young children read rhythms beyond their names? This updated version of *The Muffin Man* challenges children to read new rhythms with their old friend, the Muffin Man. The following chant will require a chorus of two sections: voice 1 and voice 2. Notice that the second voice has a long pattern which recurs throughout the piece. Practice each section separately before putting them together. Many first graders who know their part well will be able to chant it against a differing rhythm. It may help to give the children written scores or a printed chart to keep them focused. One child may wish to point to the notation as the group reads its part.

The Muffin Man

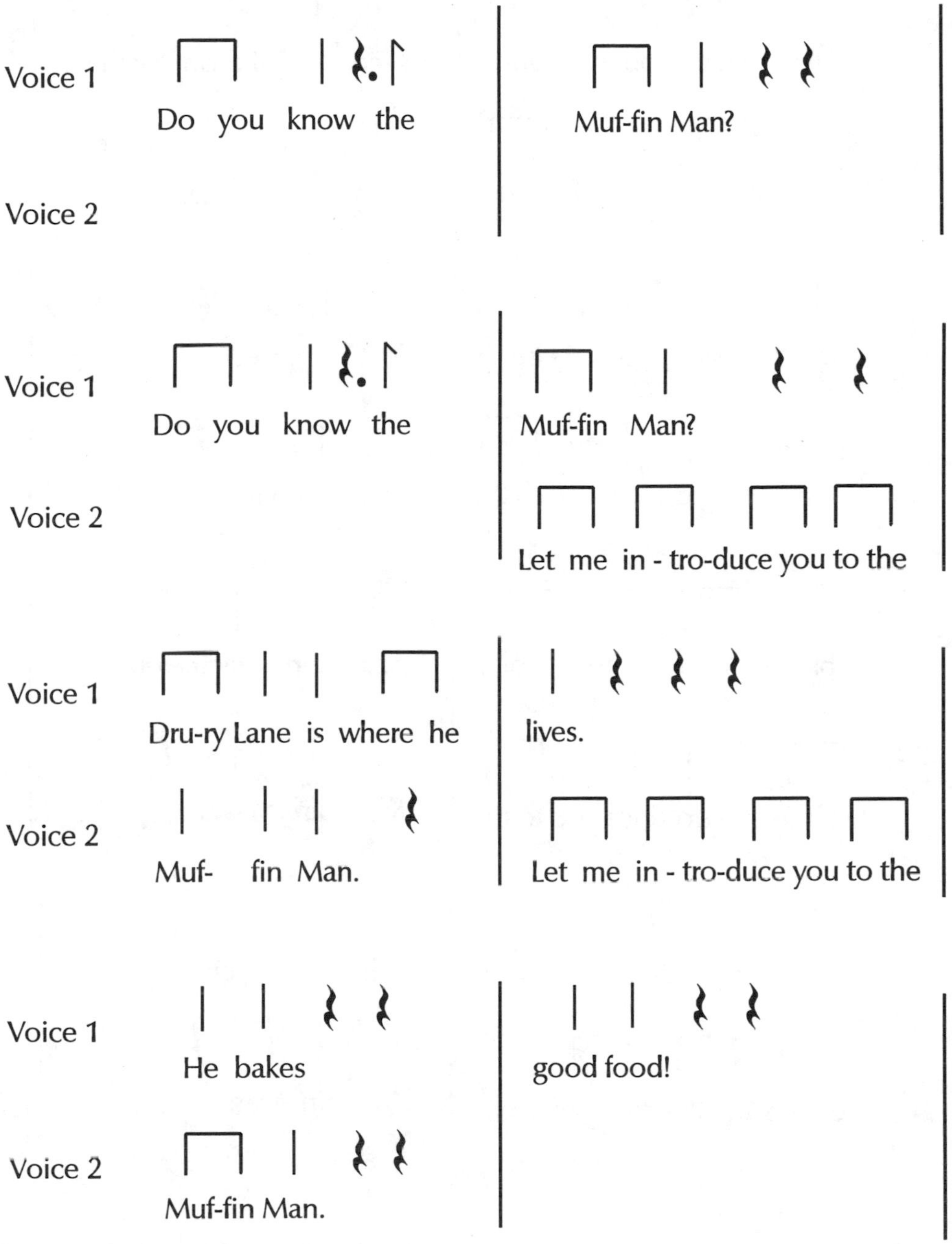

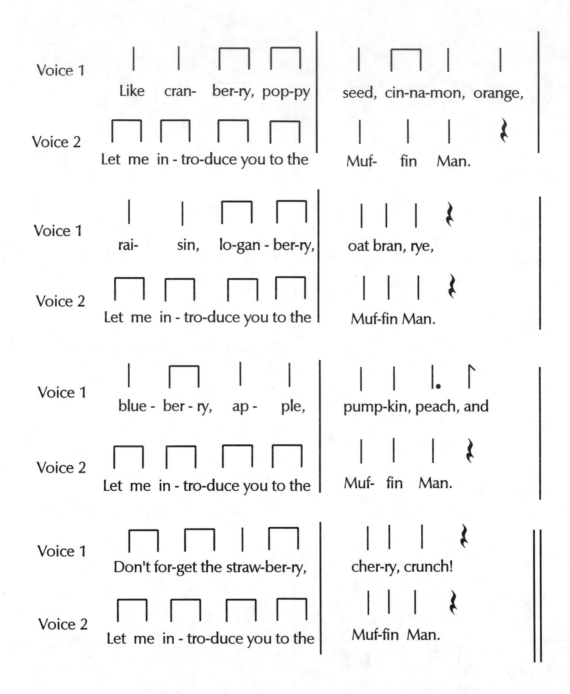

Perhaps the children will know additional stories which can be broken down into rhythmic chants. As a group, brainstorm a few sentences. Then compose a "voice 2" which will counter it. Let the children add the notation. Perform con viva!

Instruments

(Name Game)

All children have favorite instruments. Here is a chance to use their artistic talents and learn something more about the instruments that are frequently heard in films and videos.

Encourage the children to listen to the orchestral scores of their favorite films (**Pocahontas**, **The Little Mermaid**, **Fantasia**, **Snow White**, *etc*.). This will prepare their ears for thinking about the broad range of instruments in a symphony orchestra: the string instruments (violin, viola, cello, string bass, harp); the woodwind instruments (piccolo, flute, English horn, oboe, clarinet, bass clarinet, saxophone, bassoon, contrabassoon); the brass (trumpet, trombone, French horn, tuba); and percussion (tympani or kettle drums, snare drums, bass drum, xylophone, marimba, bells, wood block, triangle, tambourine, claves, and a few others). Ask them to select one of their favorite instruments from their favorite piece of music and draw a picture of it on an index card.

Have a large copy of the orchestral score ready for the children to study. This chart represents the order in which the music is presented on a full score that a conductor would use in a symphonic concert.

Conduct an **Orchestra Call** by naming each instrument and connecting it with its picture and place on the score. The leader calls "piccolo," for example, and the children having piccolo drawings come forward and place them next to the term on the chart. Continue until all instruments are "called."

Many of the scores from films children have enjoyed feature a full symphony orchestra. It is a good idea to review a few selections from **Beauty and the Beast**, **Fantasia**, **The Little Mermaid**, **Aladdin**, **Pinocchio**, and **Pocahontas** for illustration.

Orchestral Score

Piccolo	Contrabassoon	Other percussion
Flute	French horn	Harp
Oboe	Trumpet	Violin
English horn	Trombone	Viola
Clarinet	Tuba	Cello
Bass clarinet	Timpani	String Bass
Bassoon	Bells	

Advancing Skill:

★ The symphony orchestra is only one grouping of instruments. Ask the children to eliminate from the orchestral score all the instruments which are not heard in a marching band. Or invite the children to identify jazz ensemble or rock/rap group instruments.

This is an opportune time to introduce ethnic instruments that make their appearances in today's music: steel drum bands, koto drums, accordions, vibraphones, balalaika, *etc*.

Instrument Names

(Name Game)

Music notation can be extended further with games that build on earlier experiences. In this name tag activity, children are challenged to identify an instrument whose name has the same rhythm as theirs. For example, children first review the rhythm of their first names. To illustrate:

| | | ⊓ | |

Pat-rick Ma-ry Ann Rick

They should draw a picture of an instrument having the same rhythm:

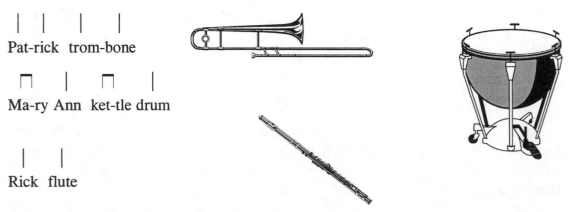

| | | |

Pat-rick trom-bone

⊓ | ⊓ |

Ma-ry Ann ket-tle drum

| |

Rick flute

On another occasion, the children might wear the name tags and take a seat in an imaginary classroom orchestra. Place the seating plan on the chalkboard and position yourself as the conductor. See the following drawing.

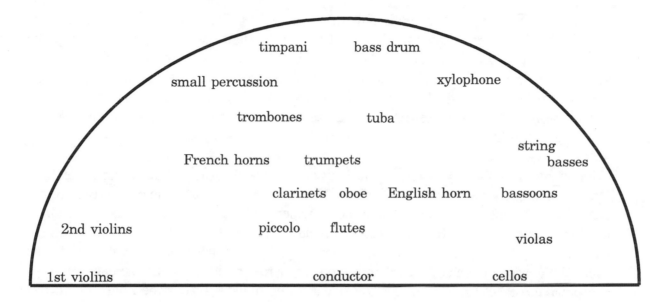

For a "crazy orchestra," allow the children to sit wherever they choose. Ask them to think of reasons why a mixed up seating arrangement might work or not work. Perhaps they can discover some of the reasons (instrument size, quality of sound, visibility, centeredness for cues, *etc.*) that traditional seating plans are used!

Frieda the Flute
(Noisy Story)

Children might be familiar with the sounds of the flute, trombone, and bass drum because they've heard these instruments on favorite recordings, listened to them as older siblings have practiced, or noticed them being played in parades and band concerts. These instruments have distinct sounds. Now, the children can identify and experience the sound range for each of these instruments by vocalizing the character responses in the following noisy story. They should use a high voice for Frieda, a rich, middle-range voice for Tommy, and a deep voice for Bennie.

Frieda the Flute — Woodwind. La, la, la!
Tommy the Trombone — Brass. Slide, slide!
Bennie the Bass Drum — Percussion. Boom, boom!

Frieda the Flute* had a crush on Bennie the Bass Drum*. Frieda the Flute* loved to hear Bennie the Bass Drum* keep the beat, but Frieda the Flute* was certain that Bennie the Bass Drum* had never even noticed her. "Bennie the Bass Drum* is too important to pay attention to a little instrument like me," thought Frieda the Flute*. Bennie the Bass Drum* was the largest drum in the band room and whenever the percussion instruments practiced, Frieda the Flute* would close her eyes and listen to Bennie the Bass Drum* make a steady, booming sound.

Tommy the Trombone* always came between Frieda the Flute* and Bennie the Bass Drum*. It seemed that whenever Frieda the Flute* was listening to Bennie the Bass Drum*, Tommy the Trombone* would sneak up behind her. "Move over and let me in," Tommy the Trombone* always demanded before taking his place behind Frieda the Flute* in the band room. "I don't know why you're here anyway," he jeered and teased Frieda the Flute*. "You're such a soft instrument, you can hardly be heard when the band marches in a parade. It takes so many of you to make a strong sound." Frieda the Flute* could feel her face getting flushed as she listened to Tommy the Trombone* heckle her.

Frieda the Flute* didn't like Tommy the Trombone* because he was always saying hurtful things to her. Tommy the Trombone* had a beautiful, rich voice and was quite conceited. Frieda the Flute* turned her head so that Tommy the Trombone* wouldn't see the tears that were beginning to fall.

As she turned, Frieda the Flute* came face to face with Bennie the Bass Drum* who had moved from the back of the band room and was standing beside her. "Ignore Tommy the Trombone*. He's jealous of you," said Bennie the Bass Drum*. "You carry a beautiful tune. I sometimes wish I was more like you, Frieda the Flute*. Let's play together someday." Bennie the Bass Drum* smiled and then returned to his place at the back of the room.

Frieda the Flute* was so happy! "I *am* a good instrument! I *am* important to the band! Tommy the Trombone* *is* jealous of me!" Frieda the Flute* practically squeaked as she thought to herself, "Bennie the Bass Drum* *has* noticed me and he *likes me*! Bennie the Bass Drum* and I are going to make beautiful music together," thought Frieda the Flute*, "and I won't let Tommy the Trombone* bother me again!"

Instrument Characterization

(Pantomime)

If the children have made instrument name tags, these may be used to guide this activity. Have the children listen to "their" instrument—*e.g.*, its special sound and range (how high and low it can play). Ask them to examine the shape of the instrument which they drew.

Listen to parts of Benjamin Britten's *Young Person's Guide to the Orchestra* for a thorough introduction to all instruments. Ask the children to imagine the personality of their chosen instrument. As they re-listen to the orchestral part, invite them to move creatively in the character of that instrument, mindful of its shape.

When the Saints Go Marching In

(Hand Jives)

Children naturally move to music. Make the most of their innate movements by channeling their energies to invent hand jives. Hand jives are combinations of different movements made by hands and arms in response to the beat. Typically, clapping, snapping fingers, bopping fists, and patschen are used in these exercises. However, taking ordinary movements, such as clapping, and expanding to extraordinary movements helps children think creatively. The teacher may ask, "How many different ways can we clap our hands?" and children will find variations that set the climate for creative hand jives.

Review the song *When the Saints Go Marching In*. Ask the children to create a hand jive for the longest notes of the song. Younger children can patschen (slap thighs) and clap more easily than snap fingers. Suggest a few patterns to get their creative juices flowing, such as:

1. patsch, patsch, clap
2. snap left, snap right, snap together
3. patsch, clap, patsch

Additional Verses:

2. Oh, when the sun
   refuse to shine.
   Oh, when the sun refuse to shine,
   Oh Lord, I want to be in that number,
   When the sun refuse to shine.

3. Oh, when the stars
   have disappeared,
   Oh, when the stars have disappeared,
   Oh Lord, I want to be in that number,
   When the stars have disappeared.

4. Oh, when the day
   of judgment comes,
   Oh, when the day of judgment comes,
   Oh Lord, I want to be in that number,
   When the day of judgment comes.

5. Oh, when the saints
   go marchin' in,
   Oh, when the saints go marchin' in,
   Oh Lord, I want to be in that number,
   When the saints go marchin' in.

Take Me Out to the Ball Game

(Hand Jives)

To contrast to *When the Saints Go Marching In*, a hand jive with three movements might be experienced. Review the familiar song or chant *Take Me Out to the Ball Game*. Ask the children to feel the beats. They may recognize that the music is organized into a triple meter pattern.

Invite the children to choose a partner and devise a hand jive that fits the triple meter pattern. Use three of the body sounds listed as a set to be repeated throughout the song. Possible body sounds to select: clap, snap, bop hands, pat thighs, "hitchhike" thumbs, or clap partner's hands.

Advancing Skill:

★ Place children in groups of three to execute the individual sounds consecutively. For example, the first child performs the first movement, the second child performs the second, and the third child performs the last movement. Suggest that the tempo be reasonably slow and begin with all children performing the sound (at different beats).

ABA Triple Meter

(Accompaniment)

The way music is organized determines its form or structure. While children more readily pay attention to music's rhythm, tempo, melodies, or instrumentation, they will enjoy discovering musical form through performance. Try this body sound piece which is organized around "threes": triple meter, three parts, and three body sounds.

Part A Clap 3

Stamp

Part B Snap

Stamp

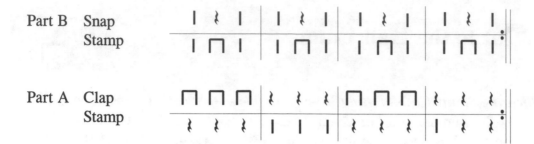

Part A Clap

Stamp

Melodic Puppets

(Listening)

The goal of this listening activity is for children to trace the melodic shape or contour of music with their puppets. This activity sharpens the children's sense of melodic shape. Most songs appeal to us due to their melodies. Children will enjoy the differences in melodies by listening for this characteristic. Using songs that children know, ask them to move the puppet the way the melody moves. To illustrate, follow the movement of the melody in *Michael, Row the Boat Ashore*:

Select songs which are not too lengthy and have some obvious melodic movement. In this collection, we suggest:

Are You Sleeping?   *Charlie over the Ocean*
Che Che Koolay   *Hop Old Squirrel*
If You're Happy   *Star Light, Star Bright*
Twinkle, Twinkle   *When the Saints Go Marching In*

Advancing Skill:

★ Expressive puppet movements are a precursor to creative body movements. Let the children select their favorite music and become the puppet to move the way the melody moves.

Beat in the Feet/Band in the Hand
(Body Sounds)

Once children have had plenty of time experiencing beats and rhythms through chants, songs, and body sounds, they are ready to apply them to instruments. Children love to play instruments for the sheer pleasure of hearing the sounds they produce. A particularly enjoyable challenge is playing instruments in a band-like setting, where everyone is coordinated and yielding a satisfying group sound.

Though many early experiences revolve around creatively exploring instruments for their sound potential and playing the instruments to the beat or rhythm, the rhythm band activity requires that the child keep the beat (as in a march) *while* playing a rhythm to a song or chant—no small coordination task!

Any songs or chants that have a meter signature of two or four can be adapted for this activity. To help children coordinate the learning of their parts, rehearse the band in stages as follows:

1. Divide the group into four different performance sections, *e.g.*,

    Group I plays drums.
    Group II plays rhythm sticks.
    Group III plays wood blocks and maracas.
    Group IV plays triangles, jingle clogs, and tambourines.

2. Ask everyone to march throughout the chant. Practice together reciting the chant and marching.

3. Clap the rhythms together BEFORE distributing the instruments.

4.   Start the students marching, then point to them to cue the rhythms on the instruments.

The following are some simple illustrations:

Peas Porridge Hot Band

Group I instruments:
(beat in feet)

Group II instruments:
(beat in feet)

Group III instruments:
(beat in feet)

Group IV instruments:
(beat in feet)

Yankee Doodle Band

Wood instruments:
(march)

Metal instruments:
(march)

Wood & Metal:
(march)

Wood & Metal:
(march)

Rhythmic Dialogues

(Body Sounds)

Before long, children will have quite a "vocabulary" of rhythmic patterns to use in creative ways, especially if they engage in these activities frequently. Each day, it is a good idea to do some echo clapping to review and stretch the length and complexity of rhythm patterns for children to imitate. Segments of rhythms from familiar songs usually work very well as echo examples. Consider the following:

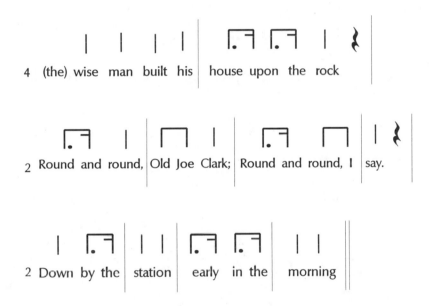

While the teacher may serve as leader for modeling early examples, encourage children to take initiative and experience the leadership role.

Warm-up

(Musical Questions and Answers)

Sometimes routine echo work can be varied to allow some freedom of response within a rhythmic task. Review some rhythmic patterns for echo work. Ask the children to repeat the exact rhythm but use a different body sound. See the following examples:

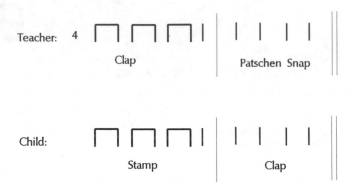

Allow children the freedom to choose "their" sound to express the same rhythm. Note these sample patterns for the teacher to use:

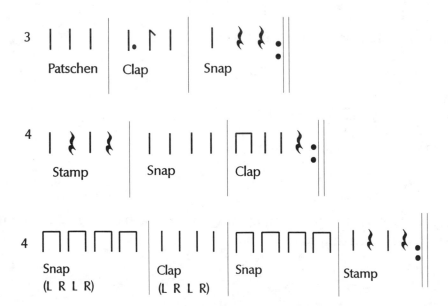

For Your Ears Only
(Musical Questions and Answers)

Many times children are visually dependent upon the leader when echoing patterns. The following activity strengthens children's aural skills in that they cannot see the leader and must listen for the pattern. They are challenged to listen for two things: the actual rhythm and the sound source, *i.e.*, specific body sound.

Have the children face away from the leader to echo these patterns:

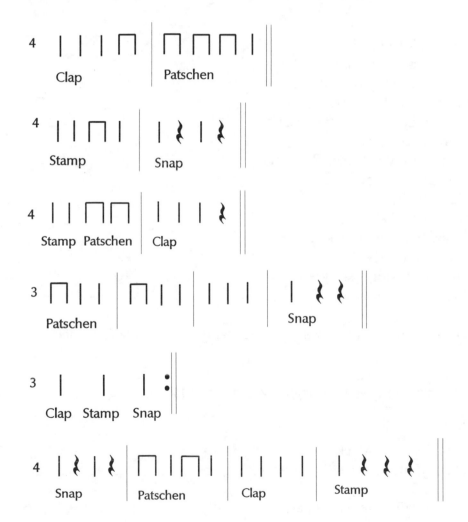

Miss Mary Mack
(Chant)

Using chants with a strong sense of beat, children will enjoy learning, then creating, their own hand jives—while maintaining an accurate beat pulse. Make sure the children know the chant well. For example, rehearse *Miss Mary Mack*, emphasizing the beat.

Miss Mary Mack

Miss Mary Mack, Mack, Mack,
All dressed in black, black, black,
With silver buttons, buttons, buttons,
All down her back, back, back,
She asked her mother, mother, mother,
For fifteen cents, cents, cents,
To see the elephants, elephants, elephants,
Jump over the fence, fence, fence.
They jumped so high, high, high,
They reached the sky, sky, sky,
And never came back, back, back,
Til the Fourth of July, 'ly, 'ly.
And that's the story, story, story,
Of Mary Mack, Mack, Mack.

Then, maintain the beat of the chant by suggesting that the children perform the following hand jive:

(after voicing "Miss Mary," begin the jive on "Mack")

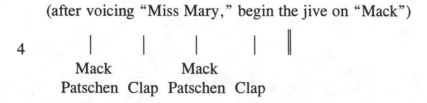

Try working the next hand jive with a partner:

2 | | ‖

Clap your hands   Clap partner's hands

With more advanced children, try a four movement jive: patschen, clapping one's hands, one's partner's hands, and one's hands again.

Finally, invite the children to choreograph their own hand jives by themselves or with partners.

Scavenger on Assignment

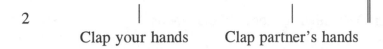

(Scavenger Hunt)

Many activities in this chapter are devoted to refining listening skills—a very important skill not only for musicians. Children generally enjoy the traditional scavenger hunts for objects. Scavenger hunts for sounds, however, are a new twist. They challenge children to find and listen to sounds more selectively.

These activities can be accommodated in a variety of environments and with modest equipment. Whether each child has an individual tape recorder, the small learning communities share one recorder, or the entire class uses a single device, *Scavenger on Assignment* will bring out sensitivities and refined listening skills.

The activities can be conducted in the classroom, however, *Scavenger on Assignment* is especially interesting when children are on field trips. A simple nature walk, for example, can provide plenty of sound awareness opportunities. In this process, the teacher takes on the responsibility for opening (or reopening) the world of sound again. Children can be made alert to a whole new realm of sound possibilities through this exercise.

Curiosity might be peaked if the teacher sets the sound stage by preparing a sampler tape for demonstration. It can model the type, length, and quality of sounds that are desirable. For example, a composite tape may include the following sounds from a trip to a forest preserve:

1. traffic noises on the bus to the park
2. bus doors opening
3. walking on leaves at the beginning of the trail
4. walking on stones or mud farther into the trail
5. birds chirping

6. something (maybe a squirrel) scampering about in the woods
7. water running in the creek

Assign children to work in pairs on this task. One can be chief recording engineer; one can be chief "logger" of the report. Ask them to hunt seven interesting sounds. They record and write down each sound. When the children return to the classroom, have them listen to their own tapes again and prepare an introduction for their presentation of the sounds for the class. As the entire class listens to each other's tapes, make a master list of the different sounds collected on the *Scavenger on Assignment*.

Band from Scratch
(Found Sound)

Recording sounds which are found in the environment readies children for found sound activities. Listening skills may be refined further through found sounds that can be manipulated. Ask the children to experiment with a sound made with an object which they can bring to school for a found sound band. Some very ordinary items can create interesting sounds. For example, scraping a piece of corrugated cardboard makes delightful washboard sounds or tapping the tops of aerosol cans results in interesting effects. The idea is to find common items to make uncommon sounds.

After children share their sounds, they should be classified in some way. Depending upon what turns up, the teacher separates the band into sections such as high/low sounds or metal/non-metal sounds. Try rehearsing the found sound band with the following rhythm patterns.

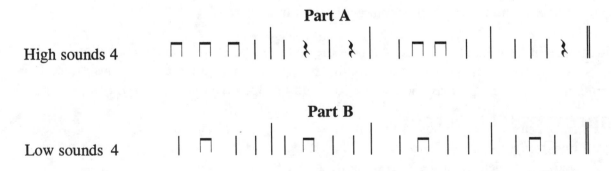

Part A

High sounds 4

Part B

Low sounds 4

If the children are independent enough to follow their parts alone, try combining both A and B simultaneously. Notice that Part B is an ostinato (a repeated rhythmic pattern). Provide a conducting or counting start.

Punchinella
(Improvisation)

In addition to a vocabulary of rhythms, children will want to explore melodies. The early explorations may build upon familiar rhythms and provide a basis for successful vocal improvisation.

Recite the following chant:

Chorus:	Here comes Punchinella, Punchinella, Punchinella,
	Here comes Punchinella, with her sound.

Punchinella: ❘ ⊓ ⊓ ❘
               Ta ti-ti ti-ti ta

Chorus: ❘ ⊓ ⊓ ❘
               Ta ti-ti ti-ti ta

With children seated in a semicircle, give each the opportunity to be Punchinella. The child who becomes Punchinella improvises a rhythmic or melodic pattern for others to repeat. After the chorus is recited, Punchinella improvises a rhythm or vocal pattern. The chorus repeats it and returns to the chorus verse.

Improvising for Grids
(Improvisation)

The next step in building musical skills involves notating simple rhythms. Rather than overwhelm children with theory they may not appreciate at their developmental level, a teacher may employ simple stick notation to represent the basic patterns. Children seem to enjoy working with the notation system used in this book. They also enjoy inventing rhythms and they need the opportunity to notate their inventions so they will remember what they have improvised. This activity will not only review their understanding of rhythmic notation but provide them with an opportunity to improvise and notate exactly what they wish to compose.

First, review rhythmic notation that children have learned. They will need familiarity with the following:

In a 4/4 time system, the quarter note (♩) or quarter rest (𝄽) receives one count. All of the following configurations are equal to one count:

Give the children a copy of an empty meter grid. See Example 1. Together, improvise four rhythmic patterns, each having four beats. Notate them in the empty grid. See Example 2 for a possible solution.

Example 1:

Example 2:

Point out that the rhythms are different from line to line and from column to column. A variety of games can be played once the children improvise and notate their own grids. Consider the following:

1. One child plays a four beat rhythm from the grid while the other figures out which rhythm was performed. Use instruments.

2. Half of the class can perform one child's grid from left to right across each row; the other half can perform it top to bottom from left to right. Are there other creative ways to perform it?

3. Select one line to serve as an ostinato (performed as a patschen) while the children clap all of the lines.

4. Children can recite the rhythmic syllables for the grids.

5. The rhythms can serve as accompaniments to songs having a 4/4 meter.

Finally, the grids can be developed for triple meter, using a nine square grid as in Example 3. Example 4 provides a model.

Example 3:

Example 4:

Creative Conversations

(Improvisation)

Children are masters at making sense out of nonsense! This activity begins with simple vocalized lines and leads to making improvised songs, extending their vocal improvisation skills and building confidence as solo singers. Using items from the **Whatnot Box**, allow the children to select one item each. Sing questions for improvised vocal response:

Teacher:

Who has the toy car?

Child:

I have the toy car.

Group:

Joey has the toy car.

Teacher:

How does the car go?

Joey:

Zoom, zoom, screeeeeeech.

Group:

Zoom, zoom, screech.

After each child has had the chance to improvise one line and lead group echoing, ask the children which lines (or objects) were most interesting. After three or four recommendations, invite the children who sang those lines to develop a small series of "events" to lengthen the song. Suggest that the group help revise the lyrics to rhyme, if appropriate. For example:

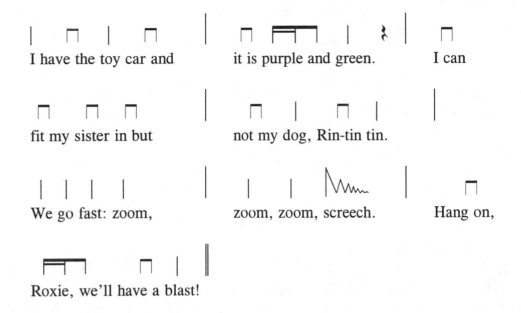

I have the toy car and   it is purple and green.   I can

fit my sister in but   not my dog, Rin-tin tin.

We go fast: zoom,   zoom, zoom, screech.   Hang on,

Roxie, we'll have a blast!

Improvisation Cards

(Improvisation)

Through the above singing, listening, and performing experiences, children have acquired some ideas about music: beat, ostinato, tempo, *etc*. This improvisatory game allows them to freely and spontaneously invent music within a very specific set of parameters.

The parameters are delineated on a chart and a set of cards which the teacher prepares, as in the following:

1. BEAT
   1a. EVEN
   1b. UNEVEN
2. OSTINATO
3. TEMPO
   3a. FAST
   3b. SLOW
   3c. MODERATE
   3d. GETTING FASTER
   3e. GETTING SLOWER

4. DYNAMICS
   4a. SOFT
   4b. LOUD
   4c. GETTING SOFTER
   4d. GETTING LOUDER
   4e. MEDIUM
5. DURATION
   5a. 2 MINUTES
   5b. 3 MINUTES
   5c. 4 MINUTES
6. FORM
   6a. AA (REPETITION)
   6b. AB (TWO PARTS—EACH DIFFERENT)
   6c. ABA (THREE PARTS—THE FIRST AND THIRD REPEATED)
   6d. ABACA (FIVE PARTS—THE FIRST, THIRD, AND FIFTH REPEATED. EACH MIDDLE PART DIFFERENT)
7. MELODY
   7a. DIRECTION UPWARD
   7b. DIRECTION DOWNWARD
   7c. LONG PHRASES
   7d. SHORT PHRASES

Prepare five or six sets of index cards, placing one item from the previous chart on each card. We suggest using colored index cards, with one side identifying the broad musical element (*e.g.*, beat) and the other side identifying a specific direction (*e.g.*, even). Color code the elements by making white cards for beat information, pink for tempo, yellow for dynamics, *etc.*

Place the children, with rhythm instruments, in work groups of five or six. (If you have melodic instruments, the melodic cards can be distributed). Give them one card from each of the seven elements. A possible combination might be:

(1a.)	even beat
(3c.)	moderate tempo
(4b.)	loud dynamics
(5a.)	2 minutes
(6b.)	AB form
(7d.)	short phrases

The group improvises a rhythmic piece using the elements of music on the cards as their parameters. Give the children six to eight minutes to prepare their pieces. At the end of the creative time, all improvisations can be shared with the class. The listening task is to identify the characteristics of the improvisation with respect to the elements as listed on the chart.

A second group might have been given the following set of cards:

(1b.)	uneven beat
(3d.)	getting faster tempo
(4a.)	soft dynamics
(5c.)	4 minutes
(6d.)	ABACA form
(7c.)	long phrases

This improvisation should sound markedly different from the previous one. With different combinations of cards, the results may vary from experience to experience. Distributing different instruments will change the experience. If no instruments are available, the children can use found sounds, body sounds, vocal sounds, or a combination of all three.

The Listener as Conductor

(Creative Movement)

The *Improvisation Cards* and chart in the previous activity can be used on a number of occasions. Children can use them to identify not only what they create but for what they hear. Adding an additional set of cards (meter) will increase knowledge and facilitate the following conducting exercise.

Most of the music the children have been singing or playing has a metric organization of twos or threes. That means if the music were to be conducted the director would move his or her arms to patterns of two or three beats. The numbers at the outset of songs or chants indicate metric organization. (It might be a good idea to review familiar songs and feel the meter as you sing them.)

As the leader, the teacher has a couple of preparatory duties to this listening and conducting activity. For best results, first choose music that is moderately fast and brief in duration.

Second, listen to it several times and practice the conducting motions so that they can be executed with confidence.

Teach the children the basic conducting pattern for duple meter, *i.e.*, music that moves in such a way that we feel beats organized into patterns of two. See illustration.

Duple Meter Pattern

Most marches are excellent examples of duple meter music. Ask the children to place a straw or unsharpened pencil in their right hands and follow your introductory count-off, which will set the tempo (speed). Give them the preparation of "One, two, down, up, let's go!"

During another exercise, a contrasting meter may be explored. Triple meter is conducted in a triangular-like figure. Follow similar steps in introducing triple meter.

Triple Meter Pattern

Good recorded examples for practicing duple and triple meter conducting follow:

<u>Duple</u>

"The Virginia Company" *Pocahontas* (Menken)
"Steady as the Beating Drum" *Pocahontas* (Menken)
"Overture" *Nutcracker Suite* (Tchaikovsky)
"Pizzicato Polka" *Ballet Suite No. 1* (Shostakovich)
"March Past of the Kitchen Utensils" *The Wasps* (Vaughan Williams)
Piano Concerto in A Minor (Grieg)
Third Movement, *Classical Symphony* (Prokofiev)
"March" *The Love of Three Oranges* (Prokofiev)
"Fanfare" *The Little Mermaid* (Menken)
"Jig" *The Little Mermaid* (Menken)

Triple

"Les Poissons" *The Little Mermaid* (Menken/Ashman)
"The Elephants" *Carnival of Animals* (Saint-Saëns)
"Toreador Song" *Carmen* (Bizet)
"Dance of the Sugar Plum Fairy" *Nutcracker Suite* (Tchaikovsky)
"Anitra's Dance," *Peer Gynt Suite* (Grieg)
Circus Music (Copland)
Mazurka in A Flat Major (Chopin)

Some familiar songs to conduct include:

Duple Meter	Triple Meter
Yankee Doodle	*Happy Birthday*
Blue Bird	*America*

If the children get "lost" in conducting patterns, return to hand jives which stress the meter patterns more deliberately such as duple (patschen, clap) or triple (patschen, clap, snap fingers).

Advancing Skill:

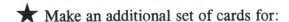 Make an additional set of cards for:

    8. METER
       8a. DUPLE METER
       8b. TRIPLE METER

Using the cards from the *Improvisation Cards* exercise, allow teams of children (5–6) to match elements of music to the piece conducted.

What's the Same? What's Different?
(Listening)

The object of this lesson is for the children to listen carefully for similarities and differences between two recordings. Most of the pairs we have suggested have obvious differences. But some elements may be the same. Follow the suggested format to see if it fits your teaching style, then adapt accordingly:

Place the names of the two selected compositions and composers on the chalkboard. Below them, set up two columns. Over one column, place the heading, "What's the same?" Over the other, place the heading, "What's different?"

Listen to the music (about four minutes into each composition). Begin discussing answers. If some observations are not correct or if some children disagree, place responses in the answer column with question marks. Try to solicit five or six similarities and differences. Go beyond the factual information, such as both pieces were composed by a person whose name starts with "G." Try to find some musical similarities, such as both pieces used loud and soft dynamics. (The improvisation cards or chart would be useful for building observations.)

Ask the children to decide which composition they individually like better. Discuss reasons why. Encourage children to use the musical vocabulary often in their responses. For example, reinforce children's opinions, such as: "I like the first piece better because it gets faster and louder." Or "I didn't like the first piece because it seemed to repeat the same tune over and over again." If children provide only compliments or criticisms, dig deeper for a musical basis for their feelings. To illustrate, if a child offers that he or she liked the first piece because it was more "exciting," the teacher might probe: "What happened in the music to create excitement? What did the composer do to excite you? How can music be exciting?"

Re-listen to the piece to bring the lesson to closure.

Pairs of pieces we recommend for study include:

An American in Paris (Gershwin)
The Moldau (Smetana)

The Engulfed Cathedral (Debussy)
Polonnaise in A Flat Major (Chopin)

Gymnopedies No. 3 (Satie)
Sonata for Two Pianos and Percussion (Bartok)

El Salon Mexico (Copland)
Fantasia on a Theme by Thomas Tallis (Vaughan Williams)

Papillons (Schumann)
Toccata in D Minor (Prokofiev)

Symphony of Psalms (Stravinsky)
Polovetsian Dances (Borodin)

Prelude No. 3 (Gershwin)
Prelude in E Minor (Chopin)

Brandenburg Concerto No. 2 in F Major (Bach)
Music for Strings, Percussion and Celesta (Bartok)

Symphony No. 101 in D Major "Clock" (Haydn)
The Soldier's Tale (Stravinsky)

"Pavane for a Dead Princess" *Mother Goose Suite* (Ravel)
The Pines of Rome (Respighi)

Suite No. 1 in E Flat Major (Holst)
Cantata No. 140 Wachet auf, ruft uns die Stimme (Bach)

"Hop o' My Thumb" *Mother Goose Suite* (Ravel)
Suite from the Incredible Flutist (Piston)

"Grandmother Willow" *Pocahontas* (Menken)
"I'll Never See Him Again" *Pocahontas* (Menken)

"Hoedown" *Triology* (Emerson, Lake & Palmer (arr))
Hoedown (Copland)

"Veni Sancte Spiritus: Front Titles" *Shadowlands* (Fenton)
"Track I" *Themes* (Vengelis)

"Main Title" *Chariots of Fire* (Vengelis)
"Be Our Guest" *Beauty and the Beast* (Menken/Ashman)

"Fireworks" *The Little Mermaid* (Menken)
"Bedtime" *The Little Mermaid* (Menken)

"Listen with Your Heart I" *Pocahontas* (Menken/Schwartz)
"Listen with Your Heart II" *Pocahontas* (Menken/Schwartz)

Musical Style Show

(Listening)

Outside of rock, rap, and country western, often all the other styles of music get lumped into the broad category of "classical." According to many listeners, all other symphonic-sounding music from five centuries sounds the same and is typically not differentiated.

To help children develop some sense of musical style, arrange for a musical style show for one week each month. This is done by simply playing the music of one era for a week. The recordings can be played as the children arrive in the morning, return from recess or lunch, during the designated music period, or as an accompaniment to movement or art lessons. It is not necessary for the children to learn titles of literature, composers, or specific dates. Rather, the teacher can simply indicate on the chalkboard, "This week we are listening to Renaissance style music."

Select at least five recordings from each stylistic period and give the children the "flavor" of the music from composers who may have created works for an orchestra, a small ensemble (duet, trio), a chorus, or solo instrument. Any of the compositions by the composers in the categories which follow will be appropriate. This list is not exhaustive. It merely gives a sampling of composers whose works generally can be found in public library collections.

Medieval (1200–1300)
- Landino
- Machaut
- Perotin

Renaissance (1400–1600)
- Byrd
- Dufay
- Josquin Des Prez
- Lasso
- Morley
- Obrecht
- Okeghem
- Palestrina

Baroque (1600–1750)
- Bach
- Corelli
- Handel
- Lully
- Monteverdi
- Pergolesi
- Scarlatti

Classical (1750–1800)
- Haydn
- Mozart

Romantic (1800–1900)
- Beethoven
- Berlioz
- Brahms
- Chopin
- Faure
- Liszt
- Mendelssohn
- Mussorgski
- Puccini
- Rachmaninoff

Romantic (cont'd.)
- Rimsky-Korsakov
- Saint-Saëns
- Schumann
- Tchaikovsky
- Verdi
- Wagner

Twentieth Century
- Bartok
- Berg
- Bernstein
- Bloch
- Copland
- Debussy
- Dvorak
- Gershwin
- Grieg
- Grofe
- Honegger
- Ives
- Joplin
- Milhaud
- Prokofiev
- Ravel
- Satie
- Still
- Stravinsky
- Thompson (Virgil)
- Thompson (Randall)
- Vaughan Williams
- Villa-Lobos

Contemporary
Kenny G
Alan Menken
Stephen Sondheim
Vengelis
John Williams

Modern Arrangements of Classical Works By
Blood, Sweat & Tears
Emerson, Lake & Palmer

Music Connections

(Listening and Moving)

Once children readily identify melodies, they can focus on finer aspects of those melodies that create special effects. One expressive element of music is the way in which the musical tones are related to one another. In a melody, sometimes the notes are smoothly connected. Other times they might be distinctly detached. In a rhythm, the notes can be even and regular or they can be uneven, choppy, and jerky. Having something concrete to move (like a puppet or body) shows others how the child perceives note relationships.

To prepare for the *Music Connections* exercise, have the children design a stick puppet. The figure or object they draw, paint/color, and cut out should be stapled to the top of a straw or pasted on a small wooden stick. (These puppets can be used for a variety of creative exercises, and you may wish to laminate their art work so their usage can be extended throughout the school year.)

Have the children listen to some recorded music (a segment of no more than 3–5 minutes) while *planning* to move their puppets. Then, re-listen and ask the children to show you how even or uneven the rhythm is through puppet movements. A third listening might involve moving the puppets the way the melody notes are connected (smooth or choppy). The more the children listen, the more they can derive from the music. Therefore, do not hesitate to use the same musical example many times over.

Here are some examples that have strong contrasts:

Fanfare for the Common Man (Copland)
Prelude to an Afternoon of a Faun (Debussy)

"Fetes" *Nocturnes* (Debussy)
"Nuages" *Nocturnes* (Debussy)

"Fossils" *Carnival of Animals* (Saint-Saëns)
"Swan" *Carnival of Animals* (Saint-Saëns)

"Ship at Sea" *Pocahontas* (Menken)
"Under the Sea" *The Little Mermaid* (Menken/Schwartz)

"Fathoms Below" *The Little Mermaid* (Menken/Ashman)
"Wedding Announcement" *The Little Mermaid* (Menken)

"Samuel Goldenberg and Schmuyle" *Pictures at an Exhibition* (Mussorgsky)
"Bydlo" *Pictures at an Exhibition* (Mussorgsky)

Night on Bald Mountain (last few minutes) (Mussorgsky)
Adagio for Strings (first few minutes) (Barber)

Name That Tune

(Listening)

Yet another activity to extend listening skills of the children is *Name That Tune*. In this exercise, "hints" (rhythmic or melodic) of tunes are given. The object of *Name That Tune* is to recognize the song from brief phrases. The teacher might sing just the first three notes of the phrase and the children sing the rest of the phrase and name the song. Or the teacher might clap the rhythm of the first phrase, with the child clapping the second phrase and naming the song.

Beware that some tunes share the same opening tones and some songs have the same rhythms (*Happy Birthday* and *The Star Spangled Banner*). "Proof" children's responses by asking, "How could you tell?" or "Are there any other songs we know that have the same (similar) rhythm?" To assure some success, select songs the children have been singing recently.

Chapter 3

HEALTH

Content	Music/Creative Drama	
Traffic Safety	Name Game:	Safety Signs
	Creative Movement:	Safety Signals
Nutrition	Finger Play:	Breakfast
	Noisy Story:	A Good Breakfast
	Pantomime:	Marie, Who Would Not Eat Her Vegetables
	Name Game:	Food Groups
Basic Emotions	Song:	If You're Happy and You Know It
	Pantomime:	Does Anyone Else Ever Feel This Way?
	Song:	I've Got That Happy Feeling
Handling Illness	Noisy Story/Rhythm Instruments:	Davey Has an Allergy
	Choral Reading/ Orchestration:	May I Stay Home from School Today?
Cleanliness/Hygiene	Body Sounds:	Healthy Me
	Hand Jive:	Hands Off Germs
Functions of Hospitals	Pantomime:	Hospital Workers
Family Relationships	Song:	Over the River
Getting Along with Others	Concentration Game:	Ms. Rosa
	Listening:	Mars vs. Venus
Manners	Pantomime:	Ill Manners Mike
Personal Health and Safety	Circle Game:	Oh, No, Pat
	Quieting Activity:	Going to Bed

ealth instruction is increasingly important at the primary level. In this chapter the activities draw upon music and creative drama to reinforce safety rules, to explore emotionally healthy responses, or to develop greater understanding of family roles and relationships. Within the parameters of creative expression, children can explore personal boundaries.

Safety Signs

(Name Game)

Important safety signs can be introduced on name tags. Ask the children to color their name tags according to the signage colors used nationally.

Safety Signals

(Creative Movement)

Prepare a dozen or so safety signs or stop light tags the size of name tags. Vary the signals to include such safety messages as "Reduce speed ahead," "Dangerous curves," "No stopping or standing," "Stop," "20 M.P.H.," "Yield," and wavy lines for road pathways. Distribute the signs to selected children and give them numbers. Call the numbers and ask the respective child to show his or her safety sign. The children then respond according to the sign's directive.

Breakfast

(Finger Play)

Starting the day with a good breakfast is an important lesson for young children to learn, and this finger play serves as a delightful aid to understanding. After playing, encourage the children to identify their favorite breakfast foods.

The morning is a quiet time.	(finger to lips to "sssh")
My Mommy's still asleep.	(rest head on folded hands)
When to the breakfast table, I	
So quietly do creep.	(walk in place on tiptoe)
I eat a muffin and some fruit	(pantomime eating)
To stop my tummy's noise.	(rub tummy)
Breakfast is an important meal	(nod head)
For growing girls and boys.	(move flat hand upward)
"Would you like juice?" I hear a voice,	(cup hand to ear)
"I'll gladly pour a cup."	(pantomime pouring)
"Oh, yes!" I answer happily.	(nod head rapidly)
My Mommy's finally up!	(blow kiss)

Advancing Skill:

★Replay as a narrative pantomime poem. When playing as a poem, ask the children to play in pairs, with one assuming the role of Mommy and the other the role of the child.

A Good Breakfast

(Noisy Story)

Build upon the importance of a good, nutritious breakfast introduced in the previous finger play. First graders can go from the finger play to this noisy story directly, while second graders will prefer coupling *Breakfast* enacted as a narrative pantomime poem with this activity.

As with other noisy stories, the children should be in groups, each having an assigned character and sound. Each time the group's character is mentioned in the story, they make that sound. Here, for example, the children in the *Eggs* group will say "scrambled" loudly every time *Eggs* are mentioned in the story. If students need extra guidance in remembering cues, the teacher might make the sounds along with the girls and boys. For this story, try forming five groups for individual characters/sounds and having the entire class select two characters/sounds to play in unison.

Jessica — Big and strong	Mom — Eat your breakfast
Juice — Freshly squeezed	Eggs — Scrambled
Toast — Pop up	Milk — C-c-c-old
Breakfast — Good for you	

"What would you like for breakfast*?" asks Jessica's* Mom*. "Nothing," says Jessica*, "I'm not hungry." "You must eat breakfast*," says Mom*, "so that you can grow big and strong." Jessica* thinks about this for a moment. Jessica* wants to grow big and strong. "Mom*," Jessica* says, "I would like some orange juice*." Mom* pours Jessica* a tall glass of orange juice*. "Jessica*, I am going to fix you some toast*. I also want you to eat some cereal or eggs*. Would you prefer cereal or eggs*?" "I would like some wheat toast* with my orange juice*. I would also like some scrambled eggs*." Mom* prepares Jessica's* toast* and eggs*. "Jessica*," Mom* asks, "would you like some milk* to drink?" Jessica* tells Mom* that she is drinking her orange juice* but that she would also like some milk*. "May I have some chocolate milk*?" she asks. Mom* smiles. "Of course, you may have some chocolate milk*." Jessica* sits down at the table and begins to eat her breakfast*. Jessica* knows that having orange juice*, toast*, eggs*, and milk* for breakfast* will help her to grow big and strong. "Mom*," says Jessica*, "I like having orange juice*, toast*, eggs*, and milk* for breakfast*. This tastes good!"

Replay this story by substituting rhythm instruments or found sounds for the food in the story. What makes a "pop up" sound like toast? What can be used to represent the sounds of juice, eggs, and milk? In your replay, divide the class into groups and assign roles. Those children responding for Jessica and Mom should say their sounds. Those responding as foods should play their sounds. Whenever "breakfast" appears in the story, all of the foods should play their sounds together.

Marie, Who Would Not Eat Her Vegetables
(Pantomime)

Just as it is important for children to eat a good breakfast, they should also eat their vegetables. There are bound to be those in your class, however, who identify with Marie in this poem. After sharing the narrative with the children, engage them in discussion, focusing upon characterization. Who is the speaker? How old is Marie? Does the speaker's emotion change during the poem? In what actions might the speaker engage? In what actions might Marie engage? Should the speaker offer Marie a treat for eating her vegetables? What else could the speaker do to get Marie to eat? Following the discussion, play the poem as a narrative pantomime.

> Eat your vegetables, sweet Marie.
> Have a green bean. Have a pea.
>
> Unclench your teeth and take a bite.
> Perhaps you'll like it. You just might.
>
> Come, come, Marie, now do not fuss.
> Just one bite of asparagus.
>
> Or cauliflower or broccoli.
> Would you prefer some celery?

A crunchy carrot might appeal.
My sweet Marie, let's make a deal.

If you will corn or mushrooms eat,
I think I know a special treat.

That's a good girl. Now, open wide.
Let's get those vegetables inside.

Advancing Skill:

★ Improvise a scene with dialogue based upon the following givens.

Who: Marie, Mother
What: Mother wants Marie to eat her vegetables but Marie does not want to eat them.
Where: Their kitchen
When: Meal time

Food Groups
(Name Game)

Gr.
1-2

Identifying and classifying groups of foods in the food pyramid are skills youngsters can enjoy through this game. On cardstock paper, have the children draw or paint pictures of their favorite foods from each food group. After discussing which foods belong to each group, ask them to choose their best example, cut it out, and staple it to a straw for a puppet.

Sitting in a large circle, ask children to keep the beat with their puppets by tapping them quietly on the floor. Feel the beats in sets of two (signified by the meter number at the start of the chant). To the beat, chant the following rhyme:

2 | | ⊓ |

    Foods, foods, foods are fine.

⊓ | ⊓ |

You say yours; I'll say mine.

Each child then states his/her name and selected food with one beat rest between the two words. For example,

2   ⊓ ⌇ ⊓ ⌇

Sher-ry (rest) yo-gurt (rest)

⊓⊓ ⌇ | ⌇

Jo-shu-a (rest) grapes (rest)

⊓ ⌇ | ⌇

Lu-cy (rest) rice (rest)

| ⌇ | ⌇

Mark (rest) corn (rest)

To close the rhyme, chant the following:

> Foods, foods, foods are fine.
> You've said yours and I've said mine.

On another occasion, ask the children to classify foods into food groups. For example, in the above chant, the group would answer Sherry's chant with "dairy" as below:

Group: Foods, foods, foods are fine.
             You say yours; I'll say mine.

⊓ ⌇ ⊓ ⌇

Sherry: Sher-ry (rest) yo-gurt (rest)

⊓ ⌇

Group: Dairy (rest)

Joshua: Jo-shu-a (rest) grapes (rest)

Group: Fruits (rest)

Again, keep the beat with each child entering on time and the group identifying the food group accurately on time without "losing" the beat. For a challenge, allow the children to have five food puppets and have them change their puppets from verse to verse. Vary the tempo. It keeps the children listening carefully. Close the chant with the rhyme:

> Food groups, food groups are just fine.
> We know them well and all in time!

If You're Happy and You Know It
(Song)

Children are typically uninhibited in expressing their emotions. This song encourages them to explore various ways to channel their feelings and act appropriately within the emotional response. Happiness is one emotion and this song suggests three additional ways to show it.

Additional Verses:

2. If you're happy and you know it, stamp your foot, *etc.*
3. If you're happy and you know it, nod your head, *etc.*
4. If you're happy and you know it, turn around, *etc.*
5. If you're happy and you know it, touch your nose, *etc.*

Advancing Skills:

★ Make up new body sounds and movements for additional verses.

★ Take turns echo clapping the rhythm of each line. Let a child lead the class.

★ Change the mood to, "If you're sad and you know it, cry like this . . ."

Does Anyone Else Ever Feel This Way?

(Pantomime)

Gr. 1-2

We have watched young people display a range of emotions on their faces when asked to show how they feel. Pantomime, like singing, is a powerful vehicle for expressing feelings.

This pantomime can be played in one of two ways. One method is to have a child sit facing the other children. After the emotional statement has been narrated, the child nonverbally shows the feeling inherent in the statement. After the refrain, the other children reflect that expression. In the second method of playing, all of the children create a facial expression appropriate to their individual responses to the verse. In either approach to the poem, the teacher or the students can speak the verse or the teacher or individual student can speak the first two lines and the class can, in unison, speak the refrain.

Tomorrow
Is my favorite holiday.
Does anyone else
Ever feel this way?

It's raining.
I can't go out to play.
Does anyone else
Ever feel this way?

My grandma
Will visit me today.
Does anyone else
Ever feel this way?

My head hurts.
I must quietly stay.
Does anyone else
Ever feel this way?

I'm hungry.
My lunch we must delay.
Does anyone else
Ever feel this way?

Stay up late.
Mother says I may.
Does anyone else
Ever feel this way?

I helped Dad.
What a busy day!
Does anyone else
Ever feel this way?

I've Got That Happy Feeling

(Song)

Below is another song which nurtures expressivity and appropriate responses. It can be used as a basis for discussing emotions.

Additional Verses:

2. I've got that happy feeling down in my feet, *etc.*
3. I've got that happy feeling here in my hands, *etc.*
4. I've got that happy feeling all over me, *etc.*

Advancing Skills:

★ Perform motions which illustrate "here in my heart," "down in my shoes," "all over me."

★ Change emotion, such as "angry," "worried," "excited," and so forth. Alter tempo, dynamics and other musical elements to express the emotional responses.

★ March to the duple meter. Change the march to a slow walk, tiptoeing, jumping up, and so forth to fit different emotional verses.

★ Sing the song using rhythm syllables (ta ti-ti). Add instruments to underscore emotional values.

Davey Has an Allergy

(Noisy Story/Rhythm Instruments)

This noisy story can be played in several different ways. The first time through, follow the directions for playing noisy stories found on page 12. We suggest using four groups, each responsible for one character/sound, for initial play here. As loud responses are encouraged in noisy stories, boys and girls can verbalize energetically what happens when suffering from an allergy.

Davey — Let's play	Allergy — Oh, no!
Eyes — Drip, drip	Nose — A-chooo

Davey* has an allergy*. If there is a lot of pollen in the air, Davey's* eyes* water and his nose* gets stuffy and runny. His nose* feels sore like it does when Davey* has a cold. It is hard for Davey* to play outside when his eyes* water and his nose* is stuffy and runny. Davey* doesn't like it when his allergy* makes his eyes* water and his nose* gets stuffy and runny.

Davey's* parents take him to get allergy* shots. Allergy* shots help Davey* to have clear eyes* and to breathe easily through his nose*. Davey* doesn't mind getting allergy* shots. Davey* knows that allergy* shots make him feel better and that when his eyes* and nose* feel good, it is more fun to play outside.

Replay the noisy story *Davey Has an Allergy* by substituting found sounds for the four noises. Discuss with the children the characteristics of sounds they find. For example, what type of sound do we want to represent Davey? Should the allergy sound be scratchy? Can the sounds be made in a pattern to simulate dripping water? Can we find a nasal sound for the nose?

A third variation would involve orchestrating the noisy story with classroom instruments. Select four different instruments, such as rhythm sticks, drums, tambourines, and a xylophone. Ask the children to experiment with the instruments to discover their range of possible sounds. Assign a particular sound pattern to each verbal component of the story and replay.

May I Stay Home from School Today?

(Choral Reading/Orchestration)

Give the children a copy of the following poem, reading it with a deliberate rhythmic flow.

> I have a headache.
> I have a cough.
> I have a fever.
> I need the day off.
>
> I have an earache.
> Pain in my chest,
> I ache all over.
> I need bed rest.
>
> Let me stay home, please,
> You know what is best.
> Besides, mommy dearest,
> We're having a test!

Note the illnesses mentioned in the poem. Tell the children they will be "painting words" as they read the poem in a choral fashion. As a group, study the words which can be enhanced through vocal expression. For example, can we recite "I" in such a way as to feel sorry for the person who is allegedly ill? Can we recite key words ("headache," "cough," "fever," and so forth) in such a way as to portray their meaning? Ask various children to model vocal ideas for the group to repeat as a chorus.

Explore variations in volume, speed, accent, and pitch for each line. Determine whether all of the lines of the poem will be read by the entire group or if some lines should be performed as a solo.

Recite the title and help the children with a gesture or cue to begin together.

Advancing Skill:

★ Designate a specific sound to associate every time "I" occurs in the poem. This practice is called a *liet motif*. The device identifies a particular person, place, or thing. Also, it helps connect the material together and build suspense.

Healthy Me
(Body Sounds)

Gr. K-1

Desirable hygiene habits are the content of the poem which follows. Invite the children to "orchestrate" the poem using body sounds and vocal sounds. As a follow-up, encourage the children to try writing poems (four to six lines in length) concerning good health and hygiene practice. Plan a reading performance.

> Wash your hands before you eat,
> Especially if it's something sweet.
>
> Sometimes things are soft and gooey,
> Other things are hard or chewy.
>
> And brush your teeth when you're done,
> A healthy body is more fun.

Hands Off Germs
(Hand Jive)

Gr. 1-2

Practice the following hand jive before placing it with the chant:

3   Patschen Clap Snap   Patschen Clap Snap

This chant has common childhood sicknesses and reviews conditions associated with each:

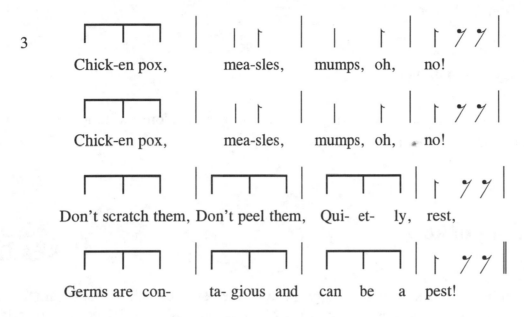

3

Chick-en pox,   mea-sles,   mumps, oh,   no!

Chick-en pox,   mea-sles,   mumps, oh,   no!

Don't scratch them, Don't peel them, Qui- et- ly, rest,

Germs are con-   ta- gious and can be a pest!

Advancing Skills:

★ Transfer the hand jive pattern to an instrumental accompaniment, as in one of the ways below:

A. Assign a different sound to each beat:

3

drum   sand blocks   triangle

B. Assign a different instrument to represent each phrase:

Rhythm sticks: Chick-en pox

Wood block: Measles

|

Drum: Mumps

♪ ♪

Triangle: Oh, no!

★ Discuss the importance of taking care of illnesses. Explore the range of common disorders (colds, flu) that are contagious.

Hospital Workers

(Pantomime)

Children recognize hospitals as places people go when they are sick and need special medical care. They may not know, however, how many different professionals are needed to staff a hospital. This narrative pantomime will help children to learn about the people who work in these medical centers. Students should pantomime an action or image that they associate with the job being described. The teacher should take special care to involve both genders in all careers.

I am a medical receptionist. I make appointments, keep records, and greet people who come to the hospital. Can you do my job with me?

I am a medical secretary. I type and file. Can you do my job with me?

I am a nurse. I give shots, take patients' temperatures, and give patients pills. Can you do my job with me?

I am a pharmacist. I make medicines for patients. Can you do my job with me?

I am a custodian. I keep the hospital clean. Can you do my job with me?

I am an x-ray technician. I operate a machine that allows me to take pictures of people's insides. Can you do my job with me?

I am a doctor. When I make rounds, I visit patients in their rooms. I try to make people feel better by studying their symptoms and identifying what is wrong. After I examine patients, I order tests or medicines for them. Can you do my job with me?

I am a laboratory technician. I run some of the machines in the hospital, like monitors, and I study cells from blood tests by putting slides under a microscope. Can you do my job with me?

I am a dietician. I make meals for the patients. Can you do my job with me?

I am a nurse's aide. I help the nurse by doing things like making patients' beds. Can you do my job with me?

I am a volunteer. I don't get paid, but I still do an important job. I visit with patients and try to make their stay in the hospital more pleasant. Can you do my job with me?

Over the River

(Song)

Children can use the following song to explore family relationships. Many children will be familiar with *Over the River* which is often sung around Thanksgiving time. Ask the children to map the melodic contour of the song as they sing it.

Give them the first phrase:

Notice that the text mentions grandfather and grandmother. Discuss with the children their extended families to include stepparents and others with whom they may celebrate holidays. Substitute appropriate terms for grandfather and grandmother.

O-ver the riv-er and through the wood, to grand-fa-ther's house we go; The

horse knows the way to car-ry the sleigh through the white and drift-ed snow.

O-ver the riv-er and through the wood, Oh, how the wind does blow! It

stings the toes and bites the nose, As o-ver the ground we go.

Additional Verses:

2. Over the river and through the wood,
    And straight to the barnyard gate,
    We seem to go so very slow,
    and it's so hard to wait.
    Over the river and through the wood,
    Now grandmother's cap I spy.
    Hurrah for the fun, the pudding's done,
    Hurrah for the pumpkin pie!

3. Over the river the through the wood,
    Now soon we'll be on our way,
    There's feasting and fun for ev'ry one,
    for this is Thanksgiving day.
    Over the river and through the wood,
    Get on, my dapple grey.
    The woods will ring with the songs we sing.
    For this is Thanksgiving day.

Ms. Rosa
(Concentration Game)

Getting along with others and helping is a part of being a good friend and neighbor. In this concentration game, students are challenged to think of ways to help Ms. Rosa. With the children sitting in a circle, the teacher begins with the following introduction.

Ms. Rosa lives in the apartment above mine. She has to use a wheelchair to get around and sometimes it is difficult for her to do things. I like to visit Ms. Rosa and to help her. I can help Ms. Rosa by . . .

The teacher then identifies one way to help. The next child states, "I can help Ms. Rosa by . . . ," repeats what the teacher has said and adds something of his or her own. Each child follows suit, repeating and adding, until everyone in the circle has had a turn.

Advancing Skills:

★When others are physically challenged, ways to help should be *enabling*. Students can create pantomime sentences that demonstrate enabling behaviors in which Ms. Rosa and her helper engage. In pairs, the children pantomime these sentences, with one child playing Ms. Rosa and the other playing her helper.

★Use the introduction as the beginning of an open-ended story. Create and complete the story orally or through dramatization.

Mars vs. Venus
(Listening)

Many ascribe music's power to its emotional content. Even with young children, music can be emotionally powerful. This activity involves listening and writing in sound journals. Using Gustav Holst's *Planets*, have the children listen to two short segments: "Mars" and "Venus." The dramatic content in each piece contrasts sharply with the other. In their sound journals, invite the children to describe each character separately, using the music as the basis of emotional inspiration.

Advancing Skill:

★As a second activity, assign the children to research information on the mythological figures associated with Mars and Venus. In particular, ask the children to find out if the god and goddess had strong emotions. If so, how did they deal with their emotions? Are these behaviors positive or negative? Ask the children to create and play pantomime sentences through which these emotions can be demonstrated.

Ill Manners Mike

(Pantomime)

Contrasting good manners with rude and thoughtless behavior can be enjoyably accomplished through the following pantomime activity.

The teacher or a student can narrate *Ill Manners Mike* while the rest of the class pantomimes the character. In a replay, all children can be invited to join in acting out the verses and, although it deviates a bit from a strict pantomime format, in reciting the refrain.

Ill Manners Mike

Ill Manners Mike just misunderstood.
He simply loved ice cream. It tasted so good.
He wanted to eat just as much as he could.

Rum ti ti tum tum, rum ti ti tum,
Here comes Mike with a ten-gallon drum.
Fill it with ice cream. Give him some!

Whenever they heard of the drum, people fled.
Mike must be a monster and someone to dread.
"A mean maniac!" that's what polite people said.

Rum ti ti tum tum, rum ti ti tum,
Here comes Mike with a ten-gallon drum.
Fill it with ice cream. Give him some!

Mike bellowed for milkshakes, demanded a malt.
"Serve it quickly," he muttered, "don't tarry or halt.
If my ice cream melts, it will all be your fault!"

Rum ti ti tum tum, rum ti ti tum,
Here comes Mike with a ten-gallon drum.
Fill it with ice cream. Give him some!

Marshmallow toppings on mint chocolate chip,
Morsels of candy from sundaes did drip.
A white creamy mustache formed over Mike's lip.

Rum ti ti tum tum, rum ti ti tum,
Here comes Mike with a ten-gallon drum.
Fill it with ice cream. Give him some!

"Give me! I want it! Bring more!" Mike would roar.
And mystified townsfolk would rush to the store.
Requests that he share, Mike would simply ignore.

Rum ti ti tum tum, rum ti ti tum,
Here comes Mike with a ten-gallon drum.
Fill it with ice cream. Give him some!

Mike's mother grew tired of hearing, "Mine, Mine!"
"Upon rich ice cream, Mike, you'll no longer dine
Until you know sharing with others is fine!

"Always say please and thank you, my son.
And finding ice cream will be so much more fun.
You and your friends can eat by the ton!

"Share it with others. What's their favorite flavor?
Soon both ice cream and new friends you will savor.
Sharing is really the best kind of favor.

"Give them a spoon and a dish or a cone.
Mouthfuls don't have to be swallowed alone.
As Most Thoughtful Mike you'll quickly be known."

Rum ti ti tum tum, rum ti ti tum,
Here comes Mike with a ten-gallon drum.
Fill it with ice cream. Give him some!

Now Mike has good manners. He munches with glee
Through mountains of chocolate shared quite merrily.
The virtues of sharing he clearly does see.

Rum ti ti tum tum, rum ti ti tum,
Here comes Mike with a ten-gallon drum.
Fill it with ice cream. Give him some!

Advancing Skills:

★ Using a reader's theatre format and/or choral reading, present *Ill Manners Mike*. Cast the roles of Mike and Mother. Let the class determine how to perform the verse, the townspeople, and other narrative.

★ Suggest that the children work on a scene between Mike and his Mother which focuses upon dialogue creation. Use the dialogue in the poem to stimulate thinking. What else might they say to each other? What other behaviors might Mike have that his Mother could try to change?

★ Use an improvisational format as the basis for story creation. Divide the class into groups of two for an initial playing. Allow only enough time for determining who will play each role, what the setting will be, and if dialogue is to be used.

Who:　Mike, Mother
What:　Mike's Mother wants him to share with friends but he doesn't want to share. Mike wants everything for himself.
Where: Mike and Mother's house

After story ideas emerge from this approach, select one or two for further development. Rehearse, evaluate, and replay until a complete story can be dramatized.

Oh, No, Pat

(Circle Game)

Gr. 1-2

This circle game invites comparison and contrast related to safety in the same way that *Ill Manners Mike* does for manners. Younger children playing *Oh, No, Pat* will often surprise the teacher with the graphic consequences they determine result from Pat's behaviors.

The characters are Kim and Pat. This particular game utilizes a "good news, bad news" format. After each "bad news" addition, the group responds in unison, "Oh, no, Pat. Don't do that." One child begins by stating a safety rule that Kim correctly follows and something good that happens. The next child gives the opposite direction for Pat and adds something bad that happens. The group then contributes the unison response. The activity continues in this fashion, following the Kim's good, Pat's bad, and group response pattern.

Example:

Child 1:	Kim looks both ways before crossing the street. Kim crosses safely.
Child 2:	Pat doesn't look both ways before crossing the street. The drivers all blow their car horns.
Group:	Oh, no, Pat. Don't do that.

Advancing Skill:

★ Play the game using manners, nutrition, or other areas the teacher wishes to stress.

Going to Bed

(Quieting Activity)

 **Gr. K-3**

Everybody needs a good night's sleep. Children can show how they go to bed by pantomiming this quieting activity.

You are getting into bed at the end of a long day. Pull the covers over you. Fluff your pillow. Close your eyes and sleep tight.

Chapter 4

LANGUAGE ARTS

Content	Music/Creative Drama	
Letter Recognition	Creative Movement:	Alphabet Animal Antics
	Song:	Old MacDonald
		Farmer in the Dell
		Farmer in the Dell Variations
	Pantomime:	Letterland
Literature	Vocal Sounds:	Hey Diddle Diddle Riddle
Writing Skills	Name Game:	Envelopes
Listening Skills	Vocal Sounds:	Cartoon Detective
		Voice Detective Game
	Musical Puzzles:	Simon Says
	Body Sounds:	Persistence Game
	Pantomime:	Lazy Jack
Spelling/Word Recognition	Movement:	Spelling with People
Homophones	Pantomime:	What Does It Mean?
Parts of Speech	Pantomime:	Parts of Speech
Oral Reading	Choral Reading:	The Three Bears Chant
	Hand Jive:	Tooth Trouble
Proverbs	Story Creation:	Playing Proverbs
Sequencing	Story Creation:	Pictures

continued

Content	Music/Creative Drama	
Storytelling; Story Writing	Operetta	
	Improvisation:	Whatnot Box
	Improvisation:	"Givens" Game
	Story Creation:	Vocabulary Word Stories
		Mix and Match Stories
		Musical Story
		Sound Grab Bag
		The Adventures of Squirrel and Rabbit
		The Further Adventures of Squirrel and Rabbit
		More Complex Stories from Pictures
	Story Dramatization:	Why Birds Are Never Hungry
		My Story Is Called . . .
		The Three Billy Goats Gruff
Creative Writing	Listening and	
	Creative Movement:	The Red Pony

erhaps the closest alliance music and creative drama have is with language arts content. All three disciplines are forms of communication. Basic communication skills (listening, reading, and writing) become more expressive, personal, and interesting when children are intensely involved. The activities in this chapter include clever contexts to facilitate drill as well as innovative exercises to expand the children's creativity. These activities promise to attract and retain creative participation.

Alphabet Animal Antics

(Creative Movement)

Combine fundamental movements and language arts experience through this imaginative activity. Select one fundamental movement (such as jumping) and begin a game of contrasts. Using the letters of the alphabet, devise two different movements. For example:

A
Jump over a little ant.
Jump over a huge alligator.

B
Jump over a big bumblebee.
Jump over a small baboon.

Notice that the size cues do not always dictate the scale of the movement. See the alphabetical list for more creative possibilities.

Advancing Skills:

★ Change the fundamental movement from letter to letter. For example, the children jump for A, slide for B, reach for C, and so forth.

★ Allow children to designate the movement calls to reinforce their letter recognition skills.

Alphabet Animal Antics

A
ant
alligator
B
bumblebee
bear
C
chimpanzee
cheetah
D
dinosaur
donkey
E
elephant
eel
F
fly
flamingo
G
giraffe
gorilla
H
hyena
hippopotamus
I
iguana
inchworm

J
jaguar
jack rabbit
K
kangaroo
kitten
L
loon
leopard
M
mollusk
mink
N
nag
newt
O
owl
octopus
P
pig
penguin
Q
quail
quetzal
R
raccoon
rhinoceros

S
snake
squirrel
T
tiger
tarantula
U
unicorn
una
V
vulture
vermin
W
whale
wolf
X
(use your imagination!)
Y
yak
Z
zebra

Old MacDonald

(Song)

This game song is especially fun when children wear name tags depicting specific animals. New verses with additional animal names can be incorporated, suggested by the children's name tags. The song can be a basis for additional creative ideas reinforcing oral language development.

Additional Verses:

2. Old MacDonald had a farm,
Ee - i - ee - i - o,
And on that farm he had some ducks,
Ee - i - ee - i - o.
With a quack-quack here,
and a quack-quack there,
Here a quack, there a quack,
ev'rywhere a quack-quack,
Old MacDonald had a farm,
Ee - i - ee - i - o.

3. Old MacDonald had a farm,
Ee - i - ee - i - o,
And on that farm he had some pigs,
Ee - i - ee - i - o.
With an oink-oink here,
and an oink-oink there,
Here an oink, there an oink,
ev'rywhere an oink-oink
Old MacDonald had a farm,
Ee - i - ee - i - o.

4. Old MacDonald had a farm,
Ee - i - ee - i - o,
And on that farm he had some turkeys,
Ee - i - ee - i - o.
With a gobble-gobble here,
and a gobble-gobble there,
Here a gobble, there a gobble,

ev'rywhere a gobble-gobble,
Old MacDonald had a farm,
Ee - i - ee - i - o.

Advancing Skills:

★ To the music, substitute the following lyrics and review vowel sounds:

Old MacDonald had some vowels: A E I O U (small voice quickly adds: "and sometimes Y")

And with these vowels she made some words: A E I O U and sometimes Y

With a bat, bat here and a cat, cat there,
Here a bat, there a cat, everywhere an a a (short a sound).
Old MacDonald had some vowels: A E I O U and sometimes Y.

In the example above, short a is reviewed. Other animals may be substituted according to other vowel sounds, *e.g.*, long e—cheetah, zebra; short i—chick, pig.

★Spelling and vocabulary words can be reviewed through a similar activity. Substitute spelling or vocabulary words according to designated vowel sounds.

Farmer in the Dell
(Song)

Gr. K-2

Spelling takes on a creative dimension in this activity. Children form a circle holding cards which have the letters of the alphabet. The teacher selects a word which will be spelled through the game. One child begins in the center displaying the first letter and finds the second letter of the word to be spelled. That child joins the center and looks for the next letter. The game continues until the last letter is found. To the tune of *Farmer in the Dell*, change the lyrics:

Oh, we will make a word,
Oh, we will make a word,
Heigh ho, the derry O!
Oh, we will make a word.

And the "s" takes a "t,"
The "s" takes a "t,"
Heigh ho, the derry O!
The "s" takes a "t."

And the "t" takes an "o."
The "t" takes an "o,"
Heigh ho, the derry O!
The "t" takes an "o."

And the "o" takes a "p,"
The "o" takes a "p,"
Heigh ho, the derry O!
The "o" takes a "p."

Oh, we have made a word,
Oh, we have made a word,
Heigh ho, the derry O!
Oh, we have made a word.

And the word is STOP.

Additional Verses:

2. The farmer takes a wife, *etc.*
3. The wife takes the child, *etc.*
4. The child takes the nurse, *etc.*
5. The nurse takes the dog, *etc.*

6. The dog takes the cat, *etc.*
7. The cat takes the rat, *etc.*
8. The rat takes the cheese, *etc.*
9. The cheese stands alone, *etc.*

Farmer in the Dell Variations

(Song)

Let children build their own nonsense words to the *Farmer in the Dell* song. The goal is for the children to create new words and invent definitions for them.

The learning parameters allow children to abandon certain conventions (*e.g.*, a "q" always followed by a "u"). Since the children will be required to pronounce their new words, the skill of phonetics will be challenged through this activity.

Each child is given a letter of the alphabet, with one child starting the game in the center of the circle. Decide how many letters the new word will contain. The group sings:

> Oh, we will make a word,
> Oh, we will make a word,
> Heigh ho, the derry O!
> Oh, we will make a word.

The first child (an "r" for example) then selects a letter and that child joins the center. The group continues singing,

> The "r" takes an "o,"
> The "r" takes an "o,"
> Heigh ho, the derry O!
> The "r" takes an "o."

The "o" then selects another letter and the game continues until the final letter of the word is chosen. The new word has been constructed through chance—with each child having an opportunity to control the destiny of its spelling! At the conclusion, the group sings:

> Oh, we have made a word,
> Oh, we have made a word,
> Heigh ho, the derry O!
> Oh, we have made a word.

Discuss how the word is pronounced and what it could possibly mean.

Advancing Skills:

★ The children may be inspired to demonstrate new words' meanings through movement or visual art. For example, they may choreograph the term to express its definition. Or painting, sculpture, or computer graphics may portray the term's meaning.

★ Keep a list of newly invented words. As a creative writing exercise, compose a story or poem using the new terms.

Letterland

(Pantomime)

In pantomime, children should respond to each of the sights in Letterland with appropriate action, emotion, and/or sensory awareness. Their journey should start them thinking about letter recognition.

Look around in Letterland,
Its wondrous sights to see.
Look around in Letterland,
Come take a walk with me.

Airplanes flying overhead,
Babies in their buggies,
Carnivals in summertime,
Daybreak bright and muggy.

Elm trees with their arms outstretched,
Flags flutter in the breeze.
Gardens ripe with vegetables,
Hydrants, red as cherries.

Infields neatly groomed for play,
Jam box sounds fill the air.
Kites across the sky do float,
Lawns green from patient care.

Malls with shops and restaurants,
Neighbors wave a greeting.
Office buildings standing tall,
Picnickers like eating.

Quaint old houses line the street,
Riders pedal ten speeds.
Schools for learning many things,
Traffic signs we must read.

Underpass and overpass,
Voters casting ballots,
Water from park fountains spurts,
Xylophones and mallets.

Youngsters having lots of fun,
Zebras dwell at the zoo.
Look around in Letterland,
So much to see and do.

Advancing Skill:

★Plan a return trip to Letterland to see new sights. The children should contribute new words and matching sights, covering the alphabet from A to Z. They can construct and pantomime a new story or poem. Many return trips can be taken to Letterland, with each visit based upon new words and sights.

Hey Diddle Diddle Riddle

(Vocal Sounds)

Nursery rhymes and riddles are fundamental elements of children's literature. This vocal sound piece is based on the "Hey Diddle Diddle" nursery rhyme. It presents a riddle to solve among the four characters: the dog, cat, child, and cow. First, review the traditional rhyme:

Hey diddle, diddle, the cat and the fiddle.
The cow jumped over the moon.
The little dog laughed to see such sport, and
The dish ran away with the spoon.

In the following score, ask some children to recite the child's line which is an ostinato (a repeated pattern). The line repeats continuously with only a slight variation in the last measure. Assign two or three children to read the cat line. Be sure to rehearse it with the accurate rhythm. Assign two or three children to read the cow line. Finally, assign one small voice to the dog line. Help the children read their lines by using one large chart containing the rhyme or following an overhead projected image.

Notice that the characters' lines are stacked upon one another, much like notes on a music staff. The voices which are at the bottom end should speak lower, using more of the chest voice. The upper voice lines should use higher voices.

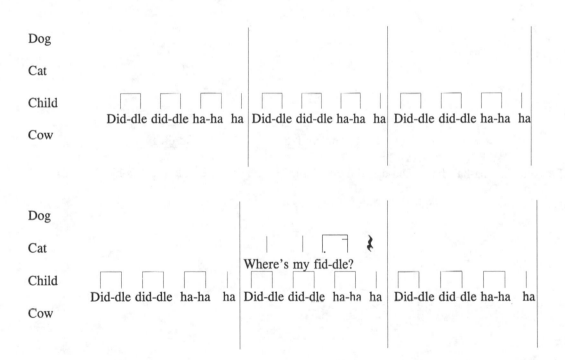

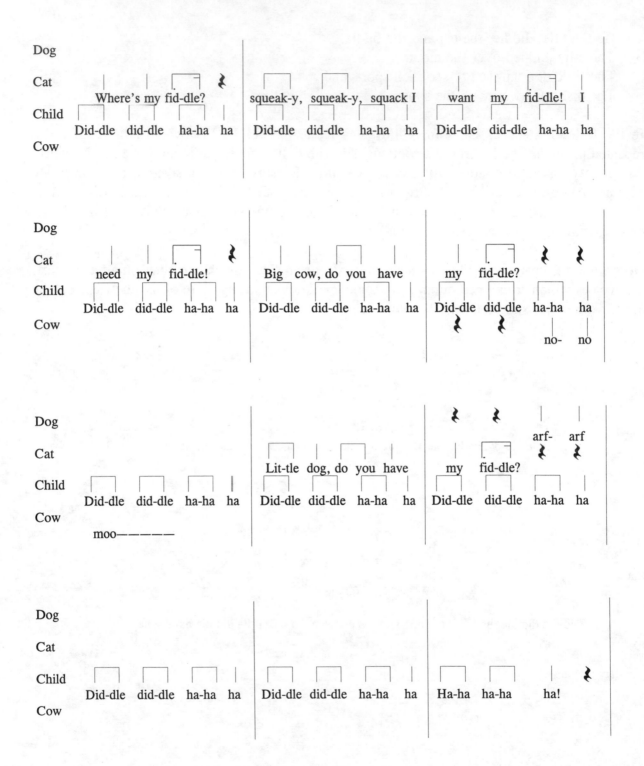

Dog

Cat   Where's my fid-dle?   Where's my fid-dle?

Child   Did-dle did-dle ha-ha ha   Did-dle did-dle ha-ha ha   Ha-ha ha-ha ha!

Cow

Advancing Skills:

★ Recite the traditional rhyme. Many old rhymes contain terms that are unfamiliar to youth today. Others are sheer nonsense. Discuss what a fiddle is. Discuss what a riddle is. Invite the children to compose their own riddles.

★ Discuss who might have hidden the cat's fiddle. What clues in the chant lead you to think the child hid the fiddle?

Envelopes
(Name Game)

Use this activity as an introduction to a research project and as a review of language arts skills in addressing envelopes. Ask the children to select a character they have admired from the past. Children will need a small envelope (3½ inches × 6 inches). They are to address the envelope to themselves with the return address from that special character. See the following illustration:

Mr. Christopher Columbus
Genoa, Italy

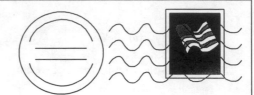

Miss Sarah Levin
9025 South Hamilton
Chicago, IL 60620

These envelopes may be worn as name tags and then used for the following lesson:

The children should look into important facts about their historical figures and include them in a "letter of introduction." The following sample might give children the guidance they need for the project.

Genoa, Italy
November 16, 2002

Dear Sarah,

My name is Christopher Columbus. I was born in Spain in 1460. Have you ever been to visit my country? I have been to America. I came on a boat. . . .

Advancing Skill:

★Children can learn more language arts and social studies skills through the following variation. After teaching introduction skills, ask the children to memorize a short self-introduction in character. Each child should investigate the costume of the period in which his or her character lived. Costumes and props should be worn for the day of introductions.

Cartoon Detective
(Vocal Sounds)

A truly enjoyable way to sharpen listening skills is through *Cartoon Detective*. Tape-record short segments of cartoon characters speaking. Keep a list of the characters. Play them for the children and ask them to identify who is speaking. Discuss what aural clues helped them know which cartoon character was speaking.

Again, in the interest of refining listening skills, lead awareness of aural "fingerprints" such as the speaker's pitch, accent, tempo, and dynamics. How do we know Mickey Mouse sounds different than Brutis or Olive Oyl? Why?

Advancing Skill:

★ Suggest that students tape-record voices of favorite film, video, or television characters. Have them lead discovery discussions to identify characters.

Voice Detective Game
(Vocal Sounds)

After cartoon characters' voices have been studied, children may focus on their classmates' voices.

Do you know your friends' voices? Can you "ID" them all? Play the game below for vocal identification. One child gets to be "Sam" (Samantha or Samuel). The child is blindfolded and circles left and right within the large circle of children.

The group chants: Circle left, Sam. Circle right, Sam.
Turn around, turn around, back again.

Sam points to a child where he or she has stopped. The child says:

You'll never guess who I am.
If you can, then I am Sam.

Sam tries to identify the child speaking. If the child is correctly identified, that child becomes Sam and is blindfolded for a turn. The game continues.

Simon Says
(Musical Puzzles)

In this game, listening is very important. One child or the teacher serving as Simon states, "Simon says," and performs a musical phrase. The phrases may consist of a simple rhythm that is clapped, a number of body sounds in a lengthier rhythm, or a sung melodic line. The children are to repeat every phrase which starts "Simon says." They may slip into the habit of merely repeating the leader (Simon) who will try to trick them at times by omitting "Simon says" before a phrase. Children who err are "out," and must hold their participation until a new Simon is appointed.

Persistence Game
(Body Sounds)

Building upon the skills learned in **Simon Says**, the **Persistence Game** poses a clever challenge. Tap out a rhythm pattern for the children to echo. Have them repeat it by clapping it, then echo it in a patschen, and finally echo by stomping. Tell them they are "stuck" on the pattern. No matter what rhythm you might perform to distract them, they are to repeat the first pattern you gave them.

For example, start with a pattern such as:

A:

Ask the children to clap it. Ask them to recite rhythm syllables as they clap it. Ask them to perform it as a patschen. Finally, have them echo it in their foot stomping. Ask them to echo it in their minds, too.

For distractors, clap the following patterns, reminding the children to answer with the "A" pattern.

B:

Return to the "A" pattern on occasion, however, and perform it as a patschen or with snapped fingers. Perform other patterns to challenge further.

Lazy Jack
(Pantomime)

This folktale has never failed to delight our students, no matter what their ages. It is an excellent vehicle for combining sequencing and narrative pantomime. As children become more familiar with the order of events and the roles, they offer engaging characterizations.

Read the story before playing to familiarize the children with the sequence of events and then cast the story. You may wish to play with one cast while other students watch, or to create multiple casts and play in unison. After casting, a simple way to sequence characters is to line them up in the order of their appearance in the story. One student plays Jack and moves down the line. Each scene is pantomimed.

Once upon a time there was a boy whose name was Jack, and he lived with his mother in a little house. They were very poor. Jack's mother earned her living by spinning, but Jack was so lazy he would do nothing but sit in the sun in the summer and sit by the fire in the winter. And as he always sat and sat and did nothing useful, everyone called him Lazy Jack. At last his mother told him one Monday morning that if he did not begin to work for his food, she would turn him out of the house to feed himself as best he could.

So Jack went out and went to work the next day for a neighbor who paid him a penny. But on his way home Jack lost the penny.

"You stupid boy," said his mother, "you should have put it in your pocket."
"I'll do that next time," said Jack.

Well, the next day Jack went out again and went to work for a milkman who gave him a little bucket of milk for his day's work. Jack took the bucket and put it into his pocket. It splashed around as he walked, and it was all gone before he got home.
"Dear me!" said Jack's mother when she saw his wet jacket and the good milk all gone. "You should have carried it on your head."
"I'll do that next time," said Jack.

The next day Jack went to work for a grocer who gave him a soft cheese for his day's work. In the evening, Jack took the cheese and went home with it on his head. By the time he got home, the cheese had melted. Part of it was lost, and part matted into Jack's hair.
"You silly," said Jack's mother, "you should have carried it carefully in your hands."
"I'll do that next time," said Jack.

Now the next day Jack went out and went to work for a baker who would not give him anything for his day's work but a large tomcat. Jack took the cat and began carrying it very carefully in his hands. But before long, the cat had scratched him so badly that he had to let it go.
When he got home, his mother said to him, "You poor fool, you should have tied it with a string and pulled it along after you."
"I'll do that next time," said Jack.

The next day Jack went to work for a butcher who paid him with a piece of beef. Jack took the beef, tied it to a string, and pulled it after him. He pulled it in the dirt, so that by the time he got home the meat was not fit to eat. His mother was especially angry with him this time, for the next day was Sunday, and they would have to have cabbage for their dinner.

"You ninny," Jack's mother said to her son, "you should have carried it on your shoulder."

"I'll do that next time," said Jack.

Well, when Monday came, Lazy Jack went out once more and went to work for a farmer, who gave him a donkey for his trouble. Although Jack was strong, he found it hard to hoist the donkey on his shoulders, but at last he did it and began walking slowly home.

Along the road he passed a house where a rich man lived with his only daughter, a very beautiful girl. But this beautiful girl had never laughed in her life, not once. So her father had said that any man who made her laugh would be her husband. Now the beautiful girl just happened to be looking out of the window as Jack came by with the donkey on his shoulders. The poor beast had its legs sticking up in the air, and it was kicking and hee-hawing with all of its might. The sight was so funny she burst out laughing, and she laughed and laughed and laughed some more. Her father was overjoyed, and he kept his promise by marrying her to Lazy Jack. So Jack became a rich gentleman and never had to do another day's work. He and his wife lived in a large house very happily, and Jack's mother came and lived there, too.

Mitchell Motomora, *Lazy Jack and the Silent Princess*, Milwaukee: Raintree Publishers, 1989.

Advancing Skills:

★ Once children are familiar with the story, they enjoy moving from pantomime to incorporating speech. The repetitive, "I'll do that next time," can either be spoken by Jack or by the entire class. Given satisfactory levels of interest and ability, students can create dialogue for their characters and act out the story.

★ Children can create a new story which depicts Jack's life after his marriage. The sequence of events in the new story can be identified and then the new story dramatized.

Spelling with People
(Movement)

Spelling lessons can be mundane when done traditionally. When students' bodies are used in lieu of paper and pencil, however, the lessons become much more interesting. Be sure to build in thinking time when using this nontraditional approach to spelling. Our students have always appreciated having time to experiment with upper- and lowercase letters, number of people needed, and audience perception of letters.

In this activity, children physically manipulate others, recognizing responsible and safe choices while engaging in a creative approach to spelling. A student uses as many classmates as desired to form letters of the alphabet and to make words with bodies. A child might call on three classmates, for example, to form her name—Ann. One student would physically make an "A" and each of the other two would make an "n." Students may take vertical or horizontal positions, kneel, work with a partner to form a letter, and so on. Parameters are based upon what is physically possible and the ability of viewers to accurately identify the letters formed. Through this activity, students experience letter shapes and letter/word recognition while the teacher gains an opportunity to check letter formation and spelling accuracy. Once students have successfully spelled their names, they may want to try a variation and physically form words from their spelling lessons.

Advancing Skill:

★For a further challenge, the children can generate sentences which classmates form with their bodies. Depending upon the number of students in the class, this may have to be done one word at a time.

What Does It Mean?

(Pantomime)

Prior to playing the activity, design a homophone word list with the children. Upon completing the list, the children form a circle. The teacher calls out a word and the children pantomime a meaning for that word. Then the homophone is called and the children show that meaning. Try using the following words in this exercise.

ant	aunt
bear	bare
board	bored
buy	bye
clothes	close
eight	ate
flour	flower
grate	great
hear	here
knight	night
lends	lens
marry	merry
prints	prince
ring	wring
shoe	shoo
tow	toe
we	wee
yolk	yoke

Advancing Skills:

★ Play the game using other homophones.

★ Play the game with a word list comprised of antonyms.

★ Play the game with a word list comprised of synonyms.

★ Make up stories that incorporate the homophones listed. If the activity is replayed with antonyms or synonyms, make up stories for these lists, too.

Parts of Speech
(Pantomime)

Learning the parts of speech can be a lively endeavor when word combinations are pantomimed. Just as the homophones, antonyms, or synonyms were graphically connected to images in the previous exercise, the parts of speech can be vividly joined here.

On individual slips of paper, the teacher writes a word. He or she then puts all of the nouns together and all of the verbs together in separate bowls or bags. Students draw a slip from each group and then create and pantomime the combination. For this activity, nouns and verbs are essential and the verbs must be active. Other word groupings, such as adjectives and adverbs, can be added at the teacher's discretion. See the following example.

NOUNS	VERBS	ADVERBS
cat	prowls	quickly
dog	hops	angrily
farmer	sleeps	happily
child	smiles	slowly
pencil	eats	quietly

After drawing a slip of paper from each category, the child creates and pantomimes a sentence. For example, the child might pantomime the sentence, "The child sleeps quietly." Depending upon the words drawn, the sentence may or may not make sense and the dramatization might produce humorous results. Imagine, for example, pantomiming, "The pencil hops angrily." Classmates try to guess what is being shown in pantomime, recognize the words used and identify their parts of speech.

The Three Bears Chant

(Choral Reading)

Sona Nocera, author of *Reaching the Special Learner through Music*, created a speech fugue based on the characters in the story of *The Three Bears*. (The *Hey Diddle Diddle Riddle* was a fugue and can be reviewed for building understanding here.) The fugue, a composition having three or more independent voices which enter at different times, was intended to be spoken as a chant, but it can be performed in other ways once the chant has been learned. A creative adaptation can be realized through body sounds, found sounds, or rhythm instruments or any combination of these. Children will appreciate working through the various creative versions.

Since children in third grade are familiar with the content of *The Three Bears* story, this activity will dig deeper into expressive aspects of the literature in this form. First, help the children follow the printed score by tracking Father Bear's (F.B.) line. Assign all children to rehearse chanting his part. Notice that the chant is ostinato-like. It repeats five times. What kind of a character is Father Bear? insistent? clear? demanding? boring?

Next, rehearse Mother Bear's (M.B.) ostinato. Notice that this chant has even eighth notes in the rhythm. Notice the repetition in her lines, as well. What kind of a character does her rhythmic speech portray? busy? hurrying? robotic? persistent?

Rehearse Baby Bear's (B.B.) ostinato, counting the rests carefully. Notice how often Baby Bear speaks up. What kind of character is suggested? Then, divide the children into three parts, according to the characters' lines. Rehearse F.B. and M.B. for the first reading. When secure, add B.B.

Discuss appropriate vocal levels, reminding the children that there is a reason why F.B. is on the bottom and B.B. is on the top—much like an instrumental score. Also, discuss the possible dynamics for the final four measures. There are a great number of exclamation marks throughout the text. They contribute to the spirit of the verse and the insistence that culminates in the final lines.

From Sona Nocera, *Reaching the Special Learner Through Music*. ©1979, Silver Burdett Company.

Advancing Skills:

★ In another session, perform the speech fugue with body sounds. Assign a low sound (stamping) to F.B. line; a mid-range sound (patschen) to M.B. line; and a high sound (snapping) to B.B. line. For rehearsal, children may quietly recite the chant to themselves. But as soon as possible, encourage them to internalize it and perform only the body sounds to the rhythm of the words.

★ Take an inventory of the highest pitched found sounds in the classroom. Classify other sounds as medium-range or low found sounds. Orchestrate the speech fugue with the appropriate ranges for F.B., M.B., and B.B. Remember to perform the dynamics expressively.

★ The speech fugue can truly sound like a rhythm band piece if the rhythms are performed accurately and there is a clear distinction between the levels of pitch. Experiment with different numbers of instruments on each part. For example, you may wish to have only one set of finger cymbals perform the B.B. line. Or you may wish to have only one drum perform the F.B. line.

★ Adapt a favorite story of the children's to a speech fugue setting.

Tooth Trouble

(Hand Jive)

Gr.
1-2

Poems with regular syllabication and metric measure in each line are perfect candidates for hand jive accompaniments! Their regularity of the beat makes the recitation an enjoyable encounter with literature. Read *Tooth Trouble* with this goal in mind.

> When I see the dentist
> I take him all my teeth:
> Some of me's above them,
> But most of me's beneath.

And one is in my pocket,
Because it grew so loose
That I could fit a string to it
And tighten up the noose.

I'll grow another, dentist says,
And shall not need to noose it.
Another still to drill and fill?
Not me! I won't produce it.

David McCord, *Take Sky*, Boston: Little, Brown and Company, p. 14.

Notice that the length of most lines is felt as a four-beat phrase. The beats fall accordingly (underlined):

When I see the dentist ⸜
(rest)

A hand jive with four movements will, then, fit the poem. Try any of the following possibilities:

1. Patschen, bop, patschen, bop.
2. Clap own hands, criss-cross clap your partner's left hand, clap own hands, criss-cross clap your partner's other hand.
3. Patschen, clap left, patschen, clap right.
4. Patschen, clap, thumb left over shoulder, thumb right over shoulder.

Bring to the children's attention the form of the poem, *e.g.*, the number of stanzas and lines per stanza. Study the rhyme scheme. Invite the children to compose a three stanza poem about their teeth in a rhyme scheme which pleases them.

Playing Proverbs

(Story Creation)

Our students have been challenged to think about language, how it is used, and what words really mean by using proverbs for story creation.

To play this activity, children form groups. Each group selects a proverb to use as the basis of a story creation from the following list. The proverb can be either the first or last line of the story but it must be spoken by one of the characters at the start or finish of the tale. For those with limited experience with story creation, the children can create the story together and then tell it to the rest of the class. For those with more experience, sharing their story through dramatization is recommended.

A good friend is better than silver and gold.

I'll sleep on it.

A silly song may be sung in many ways.

He who feeds the hen ought to have the egg.

When a lion sleeps, let him sleep.

It is better to bend than break.

Pride went out on horseback and returned on foot.

He who does not repair his gutter has a whole house to repair.

Where there's a will there's a way.

A lot of talk does not cook the rice.

Pictures

(Story Creation)

It is sometimes difficult for children to realize that *plot* is not just what happens in a story but the events and the order in which they occur. *Pictures* helps children to understand this concept as the activity emphasizes the importance of sequence in plot construction and can be correlated to story creation and literary study.

Show the children a series of three to six pictures which may or may not be related. Illustrations from favorite books, pictures of expressive faces, action photographs, and copies of museum quality prints are often easy to work with and are recommended. The children then make up a story based upon what they see. These stories can be shared orally, written, or shown through dramatization. To continue the activity, change the order of the pictures and invite the children to make up a new story.

Advancing Skill:

★To further emphasize the importance of sequence of events in plot construction, select two pictures from stories the children are reading or particularly enjoy. The same characters should be in both pictures. Ask the children to improvise a scene in which (1) these characters appear; (2) one picture suggests the opening of their story; and (3) the other picture suggests the ending of their story. After the children create and play this scene, ask them to develop a second improvisation, reversing the pictures. The ending picture becomes the beginning and vice versa. After playing this scene, discuss how the same pictures, in a different order, changed their story creations.

Whatnot Box
(Operetta Improvisation)

Building upon earlier exercises using rhythms, short melodies, songs, and chants, the *Whatnot Box* is a culminating project to form a creative piece of musical literature: an operetta (a short sung play).

Assemble a Whatnot Box by collecting unrelated objects and placing them in the box. Using these objects and the imagination of a few children, a brief operetta can be improvised. For this activity, the children work in groups of five or six. Their task is to select objects from the Whatnot Box and think of a plot that includes one familiar song and sung conversation. They may include dancing or creative movement, too. The challenge is for the children to weave each object from the Whatnot Box into the story line.

The children may use body sounds and found sounds, however, those sounds are to accompany the important vocal lines. Tell the children their little play could be about five minutes in length and it needs a title. They will perform their "operettas" for the class; however, they have about twenty or twenty–five minutes to plan and rehearse the whole show.

The first time through this activity, select five students to demonstrate the process for the entire class. The children who observe the demonstrated improvisation might offer additional ideas for the use of the "whatnots" and the direction of the story line. The following example occurred in one of our classrooms:

> The students received five objects from the Whatnot Box: a key, balloon, penny, ribbon, and an admission ticket. They drafted a story about a girl who used her last ticket at a carnival for a ride, but never got to take the ride because the machine broke. She was very sad and used the ribbon to wipe her tears. She kept looking downward because she was so sad. She saw something silver and shiny on the ground and picked it up. It was a key.
>
> At another place at the carnival was a pilot who was searching the ground for the lost key to his hot-air balloon. He had two friends on their hands and knees, combing the ground. The three of them devised the chant on a low tone:
>
> > Yo, ho, we can't go,
> > Yo, ho, we can't go.
> > Until we can find the keys,
> > We'll be looking on our knees!
>
> The sad girl turned in the key at the lost and found booth, and the lady at the booth thanked her. She gave her a penny for being so responsible. The girl ran to her mother and asked her for a papaya. (The group sings **Mama Paquita**.) The mother bought a papaya with the penny.
>
> The pilot and his crew checked at the lost and found booth to learn that the key had been found. They improvised a joyous chant on a higher tone in a faster tempo, accompanied with tapped rulers:
>
> > Yo, ho, we can go.
> > Yo, ho, we can go.
> > The key was found on the ground.
> > Yo, ho, now we'll go.
>
> And they got into the balloon, waved to the people at the carnival, and flew away.

Advancing Skills:

★ The story can be done in pantomime or with dialogue, omitting the singing and concentrating upon characterization and dramatic action.

★ Use the props creatively in a new operetta. The ribbon in our story, for example, could be used as a tape measure. New stories can be generated by the same group, or props traded to challenge other groups.

"Givens" Game
(Improvisation)

In the previous exercise, children experienced improvisation with a musical center. In this activity, improvisation is again the vehicle, with dramatic action at the core. In both exercises, the children's choices will result in various plots unfolding, assorted characters emerging, and possible dialogue creation.

In the *Givens Game*, spontaneity of response provides an additional challenge. This creative drama activity subtlety directs children toward literary analysis, as each deck of cards pertains to a category of information the children should consider when reading, writing, or telling stories. Improvisational frameworks are based upon "given" information, commonly recognized as "Who, What, When, Where, and How."

For this game, the teacher will need at least two sets of cards, "Who" and "What." The "Who" deck should contain the names, pictures, and/or descriptions of characters. The "What" deck should have a conflict situation written on each card. If desired, there also may be decks for "Where" (setting), "When" (time), and "How" (specifics of characterization, conflict, *etc.*). Teams of at least two players are needed for each improvisation. Each player selects a "Who" card for him or herself. One card is then chosen from each of the remaining decks. Based upon the "given" information the teams have picked, they improvise a scene, skit, or story. Use of dialogue is optional.

Vocabulary Word Stories

(Story Creation)

The previous two exercises have prepared the boys and girls for story creation centering upon vocabulary words. Fresh from practice with improvisationally developed operettas, scenes, skits, or stories, they are ready to let vocabulary words guide their creative responses. This next activity begins simply and can remain at that level, or can be made more demanding through use of increasingly complex advancing skills practices.

The children are grouped and each group creates and dramatizes a story that incorporates as many of the week's vocabulary words as possible. After all performances have been shared, it is fun to see which group was able to use the most vocabulary words in their inventive work. It is also useful to link the activity back to the *Givens Game* by inviting the children to categorize the vocabulary words. Which are "Who" words? "Where" words? and so forth. The same relationship can also be drawn to the *Parts of Speech* activity, as children identify the correct part of speech for each word studied that week.

Advancing Skills:

★Encourage the children to make simple scenery, posters, *etc.*, to use in the story and to label with appropriate vocabulary words.

★Write all of the words on the board. Rather than working in groups, have the class as a whole orally create the story, selecting volunteers who pick a word and develop a portion of the story which includes it. The entire story can then be cast, rehearsed, and performed.

★ Divide students in groups. Have one child in each group make a list of the week's vocabulary words so that each group has a complete set for this activity. Each vocabulary word should be placed on a slip of paper. Then put all of the words in a bag or bowl. Provide the groups with a story starter. For example, "Mother hands me an envelope and says, 'This came in the mail for you.' I open the envelope and see . . ." Children in the group then take turns selecting a piece of paper and adding to the story in a way that includes their particular word.

Mix and Match Stories

(Story Creation)

Children can move smoothly from story creation based upon vocabulary words to that which stems from their own art work. To begin, children draw or paint a picture that contains one or more persons and shows a specific location. When done, each child describes his or her picture. The teacher keeps a list on the board of the people and places the children have included. Then the class is divided into groups. Each group, selecting several characters and a setting from different pictures, creates and tells a story based upon the given dramatic elements. If desired, the children can rehearse and share their stories through dramatization.

Example:

Ryan's picture includes a mother and father in front of their house.

Sean's picture includes two small children in a playroom.

Shirley's picture includes a clerk, a parent, and a child at a grocery store.

Ryan, Sean, and Shirley are grouped together and elect to create a story set in a grocery store that involves two children and a father.

In this activity, the children encounter descriptive narrative through their oral descriptions of their art work. They also pay focused attention to characters and setting.

Musical Story

(Story Creation)

This particular piece of music easily engages the imagination, and we have watched as children listen, concentrate, and imagine with rapt attention. Younger children are likely to keep images and descriptions simpler than those who are older, but the music has broad appeal and evocative powers for all ages.

Invite the children to listen to a segment of ***The Four Seasons*** by Vivaldi and to imagine what might be happening. Prompt them by asking what ideas emerge from the music. How would they describe what happens in the segment? Brainstorm ideas, verbalizing images and actions the music suggests. Then, working in groups, the children's task is to create and dramatize a story built around the music.

Advancing Skills:

★ After listening to the music and developing a story, younger children can finger paint an image from the story.

★ Older children can replay this activity for each of Vivaldi's four seasons.

Sound Grab Bag
(Story Creation)

Listening and imagining are also at the center of this activity. The children should be grouped and each group given three recorded sounds, for example, ducks quacking, a motor roaring, and a radio weather report. The children are asked to build a story around these sounds and to include them as sound effects. One member of the group should be responsible for playing the sounds at appropriate times in the story while other group members present the dramatization.

The Adventures of Squirrel and Rabbit
(Story Creation)

This story creation activity can be used to assist children in understanding both relationships and story structure. The teacher begins the story and then calls on children to create the adventures of Squirrel and Rabbit. We suggest having three to five students contribute to each adventure. What kind of adventures do the characters have if they become friends? What kind of adventures might they have if they are enemies? Ask the students to compare and/or contrast these adventures. Use this open-ended beginning to see how many different adventures can be imagined for these characters.

> Squirrel and Rabbit stood at the base of the big tree, neither daring to move. Neither has ever seen a creature quite like the other. "What kind of strange creature is this?" thinks Squirrel to himself. "I wonder what that is," thinks Rabbit. Each feels a little frightened of the other.

What happens next?

The Further Adventures of Squirrel and Rabbit
(Story Creation)

The characters of Squirrel and Rabbit, introduced in the previous activity, can be used to enhance oral communication skills through the creation of dialogue. In this circle game, the children develop an adventure for the characters by relating what happens to them through dialogue. The teacher begins as the character, Squirrel, and starts a story. The next student continues the story as Rabbit. Alternating characters continues until the last child in the circle finishes the adventure. Students should be encouraged to create a voice for the character and to speak with that voice when adding to the story.

Example:

Teacher: I am Squirrel. Today, Rabbit and I are going to have a picnic in the woods.

Child 1:   My friend, Squirrel, is gathering nuts for us, but I'd rather have lettuce at the picnic. I'll just go look for some before I meet Squirrel.

Child 2:   I arrive at the spot for our picnic, but I don't see Rabbit. Where could he be?

Advancing Skills:

★ The teacher shares a story starter (see *Vocabulary Word Stories* for an example) with the class. Working in pairs, students write a scene in dialogue form for the two characters and then enact their scene for the rest of the class. Encouraging physical and vocal characterization is suggested. Memorization of dialogue is optional.

★Use the same story starter more than once, stipulating that a particular plot line cannot be repeated. On a second playing, for example, Rabbit could not be missing from the picnic spot. The plot would have to move in another direction.

More Complex Stories from Pictures
(Story Creation)

Progression to this activity will seem natural to children after they have participated in the other story creation activities in this chapter.

Using a print, poster, photograph, or picture of your choice, provide the children ample opportunity to study the work. The children must determine who the characters are, the setting, *etc*. Operating in groups, they should create and rehearse a story based upon the artwork. Dramatizations should be shared with the rest of the class.

To illustrate, our students have used a reproduction of a New England winter scene as the basis of *More Complex Stories from Pictures*. In the scene, people are walking in winter clothing through a peaceful village. A steeple can be seen in the background. The students determined that some of the people were walking to an evening church service and others were shopkeepers and customers returning to their homes at the end of the day. A story was presented based upon the lives of the people in this village. Another group of students worked with a picture from a magazine of a large group of people of various ages at a picnic. In the picture, one person is on the phone and others are waiting to talk. The students decided that the picture was of a family reunion and that the people were calling a distant relative who was unable to attend.

Advancing Skill:

★ Give each group its own picture with which to work. The result will be several different story creations. Throughout the school year, have groups exchange pictures and develop new stories.

Why Birds Are Never Hungry

(Story Dramatization)

Well versed in the skills needed for story dramatization from participating in a myriad of creative drama activities, students will now be ready to test their mettle on this story from the people of Laos, Thailand, and Vietnam, which offers an explanation for the common sighting of bluebirds around people's homes.

A long time ago, when the world was new, there were two brothers who went hunting. After the long day of walking through the jungle, they got lost. They were worried and could not remember which way to go to get back home to their parents. For many days, they wandered in the jungle. They did not have anything to eat and became very hungry.

One day the older brother decided that he had to go to find food and wood for the fire. The younger brother also wanted to go to gather water. After they discussed their plans, they each went their own way. They agreed to meet back at the clearing in the forest where they were camping when they had gathered the necessary things.

The younger brother went up and down everywhere through the jungle, but could not find any water. Finally, he was so tired he sat down on a stone to think. He tried to face in a different direction, thinking he might find water that way. While he was thinking, a bluebird was jumping from one tree to another, singing, "I know where your parents are, I know where your parents are!"

The younger brother was surprised, because he wasn't sure what he was really hearing. He stared at the bluebird and tried to listen more carefully. He hoped that the bluebird would sing to him and say those words again. He watched the bluebird wherever it went. After a time the bluebird started to sing again, saying the same words. The younger brother asked the bluebird, "Did you say that you know where our parents are?"

"Yes, I did. But this is a bargain. If you can give me three insects then I will lead you to your parents," the bluebird chirped.

The boy paused awhile and then he said, "Are you sure? If you are sure, will you also follow me now while I go to get my older brother?"

The bird agreed.

As the bargain had been set, the bluebird followed the younger boy to the clearing in the forest, where the older brother was sitting and waiting. He had been there for a long time and had returned without either the food or the wood. The younger brother told the older brother about his bargain with the bluebird. Then, the brothers left the bird in the clearing and went to find the insects. It took them quite some time, but they finally returned to the clearing and gave the insects to the bluebird.

After the bluebird had eaten the insects he said, "You boys must follow me wherever I fly and I will lead you to your parents."

The bluebird flew away, leading the two boys. They followed the bird closely, and after many days they finally got home. They were very happy, and they thanked the bluebird many times for leading them safely home.

Before the bluebird left the two brothers to go back to the forest, the boys told him, "We will never forget how you helped us. We hope that we can help you one day—to save your life, too. We will always give you food when you are hungry."

And that is why birds are always around people's houses now—because of the promise given to the bluebird by the two grateful brothers.

From Norma J. Livo and Dia Cha, ***Folk Stories of the Hmong***, Englewood, Colorado: Libraries Unlimited, Inc., 1991, pp. 54–55.

Advancing Skills:

★ Solicit ideas from the children about other promises the brothers might have made to the bluebird. What if they had promised, for example, to always bring the birds indoors during cold weather? Children can improvise scenes showing the results of those promises.

★ The children can find other folktales which explain common occurrences and dramatize these.

My Story Is Called . . .

(Story Dramatization)

A title is usually the last thing given to a story or speech because it stems from the content it describes. Children can have a lot of fun reversing this process and making their dramatic content fit the title in this next activity, which incorporates both story creation and story dramatization. After playing, building in discussion time so that children may share their feelings about this upside down approach to titling tales is a useful practice.

Working in small groups, children select a title for their story *before* undertaking its creation. Their story should then make sense in terms of the title they've selected. They should share their finished product with the rest of the class.

Advancing Skill:

★Groups each create titles and exchange them. Each group then creates and dramatizes a story based upon the title that it received. Children viewing the dramatization might enjoy guessing the title after seeing the story played.

The Three Billy Goats Gruff

(Story Dramatization)

Young players enjoy success when they dramatize this well-known tale. Simple characterizations and repetition make *The Three Billy Goats Gruff* a favorite. Our experience has been that the characters are appealing and young people involve themselves completely in these roles, especially when they have reviewed the steps in the story dramatization process before playing.

Once upon a time there were three Billy Goats who were to go up the hillside to make themselves fat, and the name of the three was "Gruff."

On the way up was a bridge over a burn they had to cross; and under the bridge lived a great ugly Troll, with eyes as big as saucers and a nose as long as a poker.

So first of all came the youngest Billy Goat Gruff to cross the bridge.

"Trip, Trap! Trip, Trap!" went the bridge.

"WHO'S THAT tripping over my bridge?" roared the Troll.

"Oh! it is only I, the tiniest Billy Goat Gruff; and I'm going up the hillside to make myself fat," said the Billy Goat, with such a small voice.

"Now, I'm coming to gobble you up," said the Troll.

"Oh, no! pray don't take me. I'm too little, that I am," said the Billy Goat. "Wait a bit till the second Billy Goat Gruff comes; he's much bigger."

"Well! be off with you," said the Troll.

A little while after came the second Billy Goat Gruff to cross the bridge.

"Trip, Trap! Trip, Trap! Trip, Trap!" went the bridge.

"WHO'S THAT tripping over my bridge?" roared the Troll.

"Oh! it's the second Billy Goat Gruff, and I'm going up the hillside to make myself fat," said the Billy Goat, who hadn't such a small voice.

"Now, I'm coming to gobble you up," said the Troll.

"Oh, no! don't take me. Wait a little til the big Billy Goat Gruff comes; he's much bigger."

"Very well! Be off with you," said the Troll.

But just then came the big Billy Goat Gruff.

"TRIP, TRAP! TRIP, TRAP! TRIP, TRAP! TRIP, TRAP!" went the bridge, for the Billy Goat was so heavy that the bridge creaked and groaned under him.

"WHO'S THAT tramping over my bridge?" roared the Troll.

"It's I! THE BIG BILLY GOAT GRUFF," said the Billy Goat, who had an ugly hoarse voice of his own.

"Now, I'm coming to gobble you up," said the Troll.

"Well, come along! I've got two spears,
And I'll poke your eyeballs out at your ears;
I've got besides two curling-stones,
And I'll crush you to bits, body and bones."

That was what the Big Billy Goat said; and so he flew at the Troll and thrust him with his horns, and crushed him to bits, body and bones, and tossed him out into the burn, and after that he went up the hillside. There the Billy Goats got so fat they were scarce able to walk home again; and if the fat hasn't fallen off them, why they're still fat; and so—

"Snip, snap, snout,
This tale's told out."

From George W. Dasent, *Popular Tales from the Norse and North German*, London: Norraena Society, 1906. Reprinted in *Stories For Creative Acting*, compiled and edited by C. Robert Kase, New York: Samuel French, Inc., 1961, pp. 30–31.

The Red Pony
(Listening and Creative Movement)

The Red Pony is an orchestral suite by Aaron Copland. The suite is based upon a story of ten-year-old Jody, who lives on a ranch in California. There are six pieces that describe events of the story. Any one of them can be used as a single lesson. With young children, it is best to listen to only one piece per day. Perhaps as a cumulative experience, the pieces may be combined for a creative movement performance. Below are the titles of the sections and some guiding questions that might foster creative expression.

I.   **Morning on the Ranch**

How early is it? How can you show that it's daybreak? What kind of chores do you need to do first on a ranch? How many types of animals do you tend? Does the rhythm suggest any movements that can be repeated, exaggerated, or made into a dance?

II.   The Gift

(Jody receives a red pony from his dad and brings it to school for classmates to see.) Is Jody happy to receive the pony? What does he do to show his appreciation? Does Jody ride or walk the pony to school? What does he want his friends to notice about the pony? What does he point out? How does the pony behave? What mood is expressed in the melody? Show this mood in your facial expressions and movements.

III.   Dream March and Circus Music

(Jody daydreams about things he can do with the pony.) Where is Jody daydreaming? Where are Jody and the pony at the circus? What tricks can the pony do? Does the pony march? trot? gallop? run? How does the music achieve a dreamlike state? How does the music make you feel during the dream? Does it put you to sleep or wake you up at the end? Show these movements.

IV.   Walk to the Bunkhouse

(Billy Buck, a cowhand and friend of Jody's, walks to the bunkhouse after chores are done.) How old is Billy Buck? How tall is he? Is he tired? How can you show his size and feelings as he walks? How far is the walk? Does he see anything interesting on the walk to the bunkhouse? Does he walk at the same speed? How does the music hint at Billy Buck's character? Show this in your movements. What does Jody think of Billy Buck?

V.   Grandfather's Story

(Grandfather tells Jody how he came to California on a wagon train.) Where is Grandfather as he tells the story? Where is Jody? How does Grandfather use his hands and face to describe things? How does Jody react to the stories? Are they full of adventure? Do they scare, amuse, or interest Jody? How can we show the imagined wagon train of people moving across the plains, desert, or mountains? What kinds of events might have taken place? Listen to the music for clues.

VI.   Happy Ending

What is the "happy ending" to this story? What happened to Jody and the red pony? What became of Grandfather and his Dad? What happened to Billy Buck? What happened to the ranch? How can you show happiness?

Advancing Skills:

★ Have the children paint pictures from one of the scenes of the story of *The Red Pony*.

★ Have the children write a "Happy Ending" conclusion.

★ Encourage second and third graders to develop a cartoon strip of four or five illustrations (with text) for a chosen scene.

★ Invite third graders to write scenes incorporating dialogue for their favorite segment.

Chapter 5

MATH

Content	Music/Creative Drama	
Counting	Chant:	One Potato 2, 4, 6, 8
	Song:	Hokey Pokey Variations All Hid Going Over the Sea Tideo
	Name Game:	Coins
Adding/Subtracting	Chant:	What's the Same? The Muffin Man
	Concentration Game:	Addition and Subtraction Game
Recognizing Numbers	Pantomime:	Numberland How Many Friends Are There?
Graphs	Radio Spot:	Lifestyles of the Rich and Graphic
Fractions	Noisy Story:	Frankie the Fraction
	Concentration Game:	Fraction Facts
Watches	Finger Play:	My Watch
Telling Time	Pantomime:	Match the Time to the Action Time Pantomimes
Making Change	Pantomime:	I Help in My Parents' Store
Using a Calendar	Story Creation:	A Year of Open-Ended Stories

*T*he math skills in this chapter are approached through activities which range from identification and memorization skills through sophisticated problem solving. The representative creative activities demonstrate how math facts and numeral skills can come alive!

Recognizing numbers, counting, counting by twos, identifying even/odd numbers, adding and subtracting, graphing skills, fractions, telling time, making change, and using a calendar all concern primary teachers. This content lends itself well to musical and creative drama contexts.

One Potato

(Chant)

Gr. K-1

Simple counting is the object of this exercise. This chant is often used by children to select a person (sometimes to go first in a game) or to get a special part in a game. Teach the chant, then add the movements below.

> **One** potato, **two** potato, **three** potato, **four**;
> **Five** potato, **six** potato, **seven** potato, **more**.
>
> **My mo**ther **told me to pick this one**,
> **And you are the one**.

Each child places a fist in the center. The group recites the chant while one child bops each fist on the beat (words underlined). The child whose fist is bopped on the last word is selected.

Advancing Skill:

★ Extend the chant to other numbers. Rhyme the chant to fit the final word with that of the previous phrase.

2, 4, 6, 8
(Chant)

To count by twos, perform the following chant with a decided beat:

> Two, four, six, eight,
> Who do we appreciate?
> Bus driver, bus driver,
> Yeah!

This chant is based on the traditional rhyme:

> Two, four, six, eight,
> Meet me at the garden gate.
> If I'm late, don't wait.
> Two, four, six, eight.

Advancing Skills:

★ After learning the appreciation chant, teach the children the rhythmic syllables and notation for it:

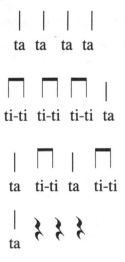

★ Alternate echoing the lines of the rhyme. For example:

Teacher claps: | | | | Students echo: | | | |

Teacher claps: ⊓ ⊓ ⊓| Students echo: ⊓ ⊓ ⊓|

★ Place the rhythmic notation for each line of the chant on the chalkboard. Ask the children to identify which line you have clapped.

★ The chant can be expanded by counting beyond eight and creating new lyrics to rhyme:

> Ten, twelve, fourteen, sixteen,
> Always kind and never mean . . .

★ Count by threes, fives, or tens and create additional rhymes.

Hokey Pokey Variations

(Song)

Using the familiar game song, paraphrase the lyrics to review certain math or language arts concepts. Depending upon the nature of the lesson, children should have flash cards with appropriate exemplars on them. For example, the math lesson requires each child to have a card with a different number on it. The children may sit in a circle and place their cards inside the circle when appropriate.

Math:
> You put your even numbers in . . .

Language Arts:
> You put your vowels in . . .

All Hid

(Song)

Many agree that if it weren't for learning the alphabet through the *Twinkle Twinkle* melody, they would not have been able to memorize the letters. *All Hid* is a clever way to learn to count by fives. It also is an echo song—one the children may lead as soon as they know their math facts!

Notice the repetition between the soloist and chorus. There also is a good deal of repetition (singing on the same tone) throughout the song, making it simple but rhythmically delightful.

Going Over the Sea

(Song)

This song was first sung by Canadian children. Like the familiar song *This Old Man*, it can be performed as a finger play. Suggest appropriate lyrics for each numeral. For example:

"When I was:

two . . . tied my shoe
three . . . bumped my knee
four . . . shut the door
five . . . learned to jive
six . . . picked up sticks

seven . . . went to heaven
eight . . . learned to skate
nine . . . climbed a vine
ten . . . caught a hen"

Encourage children to designate (using fingers) each number as the verses are sung.

Advancing Skills:

★ Ask for other movements such as jumping, saluting like a soldier, stamping on "one," "two," and "three."

★ After the words are learned in this version, invite children to think of other rhyming possibilities for each age. For example, "When I was one I sucked my thumb . . ."

When I was one I ate a bun, Go-ing o-ver the sea. I jumped a-board a sail-or-man's ship, And the sail-or-man said to me, "Go-ing o-ver, go-ing un-der, Stand at at-ten-tion like a sol-dier, With a one, two, and three."

Tideo
(Song)

Gr. 1-2

Numbers are used in *Tideo*'s lyrics. They may also suggest movements based on the numbers. Learn the song and game and then have additional fun with follow-up ideas.

Children hold hands in a circle and raise them to let a child through the "windows."

Lines 1 and 2: One child skips in and out of the circle through the open windows.

Line 3: Circle children lower windows. Child in center faces one child. On the first "tideo," the partners patschen to the pattern ⊓ | ; on the second "tideo," they clap their own hands to the pattern: ⊓ | ; they link elbows and turn so that the first child joins the circle and the second child is ready to begin the game; on the final "tideo," they clap each others' hands.

Advancing Skills:

★ On a paper folded into three panels, ask children to draw the number of windows for each verse.

★ Place the rhythmic phrases of the song on a chart as below. Notice the repetition and contrast:

⊓ ⊓ | ⊓ ı |

⊞⊓ | ⊓ ı |

⊓ ı | ⊓ ı |

⊞⊓ | ⊓ ı |

★ Ask the children to identify how many different patterns make up the song. (There are three patterns:)

⊓ ⊓

⊓ ı

⊞⊓

Count how many times each pattern is repeated.

★ Try each one of the three patterns as an ostinato (a repeated figure) to accompany the song. Suggested instruments are:

rhythm sticks: ⊞ ⊓

drums: ⊓ ı

jingle clogs: ⊓ ⊓

★ Invite the children to create a different body sound pattern for each rhythm used in the song, for example:

patschen   clap

★ Perform the song with "intermissions." After singing the first two measures, allow the children to choreograph movements which illustrate the number of windows. For example, after passing one window, one movement is inserted after "tideo," after passing two windows, two movements are supplied after "ti-de-o," and so forth. Pass as many windows as the children can handle.

Coins
(Name Game)

This exercise reinforces coin recognition and counting by fives and tens. Make name tags that look like coin denominations. Children can learn to count by fives and tens when everyone has a "nickel" name tag or a "dime" name tag. Sing *All Hid* for clever integration of math facts.

Form two circles of children, placing "dimes" in a concentric circle within the nickels. Every time reference to a nickel or fives is mentioned, the nickels do a knee bend. Similarly, every time the dime or multiples of ten are mentioned, the dimes do a knee bend. Ask the inner circle to face outward for another variation, taking care not to be confused by the outer circle's actions.

What's the Same?
(Chant)

With the children seated in a circle, use a patschen (patting thighs) to establish the beat. Begin the chant. The group speaks the opening of the chant in unison. Moving around the circle, one child then states his or her name and an addition or subtraction equation using the numbers one through twelve. The next child says his or her name and a balancing equation. The third child states his or her name and a new equation and the fourth child continues with name and balancing equation. This continues until all children have participated. The group then ends the activity by repeating the opening of the chant in unison. Throughout the exercise, keep the beat of the chant. If this is lost or if a math equation is incorrect, stop and begin again with the opening verse and new equations. The teacher should decide whether to immediately rectify an incorrect equation or to postpone the correction.

Example:

(Chant)	What is equal?
	What's the same?
	Learn the numbers.
	Learn the names.

Jonah:	Jonah. Three and six are nine.
Carlos:	Carlos. Eight and one are nine.
Juanita:	Juanita. Six minus four is two.
Ian:	Ian. Five minus three is two.

What is equal?
What's the same?
Learn the numbers.
Learn the names.

The Muffin Man
(Chant)

Children can create their own addition problems through varying a chant's lyrics. Review the familiar chant:

> Oh, do you know the muffin man, the muffin man, the muffin man?
> Oh, do you know the muffin man, who lives in Drury Lane?

Substitute math facts for "the muffin man." For example, "Do you know three plus four, three plus four, three plus four? Do you know three plus four, who has the answer now?"

The child who answers correctly then creates a new problem to be chanted.

Addition and Subtraction Game
(Concentration Game)

The previous chants serve as appropriate warm ups for this concentration game. Until children become proficient with this activity, we recommend playing it in groups of five or six. Later, group size can be enlarged.

The children sit in a circle and the first child states and solves an addition or subtraction problem. The child to his or her left must restate the problem and then add a new one. This continues around the circle, with each child repeating the previous problems before adding a new one. Children may assist classmates who have difficulty remembering. If the children remember the problems easily, they may wish to go around the circle another time with new problems.

Example:

> Child 1: Four and five are nine.

> Child 2: Four and five are nine. One and two are three.

> Child 3: Four and five are nine. One and two are three. Two minus one is one.

Numberland

(Pantomime)

In the Language Arts chapter, the children visit Letterland to gain experience with letter recognition. Following the directions for that activity, take a trip to Numberland with the boys and girls in your class. After pantomiming the entire poem in unison, replay with only the number called for to execute each character and action. One child, for example, would play the newspaper carrier, three children would play jump rope, and so forth. This replay provides visual representation of the numbers.

Look around in Numberland.
Its wondrous sights to see.
Look around in Numberland.
Come look and count with me.

One newspaper carrier
Delivering each day,
Walk by the mosque and temple,
Two places people pray.

Three children playing jump rope,
Let's join them as they twirl.
Beauticians busy styling,
Four customers need curls.

Five painters changing houses
From colors dull to bright.
Making our breakfast donuts,
Six bakers work at night.

Seven riders on the bus
Do travel through the town.
Escalators at the mall,
Eight folks move up and down.

Nine men repair the sidewalk
So we can safely walk.
Stop at the local diner,
Ten people eat and talk.

Look around in Numberland.
Its wondrous sights to see.
Look around in Numberland.
We're counting happily.

Advancing Skill:

★ Children can take return trips to Numberland often, pantomiming new characters and sights they've invented for numbers one through ten.

How Many Friends Are There?

(Pantomime)

This activity combines pantomime with oral responses to math problems. The teacher may select students to enact each problem or cast from volunteers. Every statement should have its own cast. Each statement ends with a math question to which all children respond orally.

Suggested Statements:

Four friends are playing basketball. Two more children join them. How many people are playing basketball?

Two friends are taking a walk. Another friend joins them. How many friends are taking a walk?

Ten friends are building a snowman. Five friends decide to go sledding instead. How many friends are still building a snowman?

Six friends are playing on the swings in the park. Three friends leave the swings and play on the slide. How many friends are playing on the swings?

Seven friends are having a slumber party. Three go from the bedroom to the living room to watch a video. How many friends are still in the bedroom?

Five friends are riding their bicycles. Two are called home for dinner. How many friends are still riding bicycles?

Three friends are playing with a puppy. Two friends join them. How many friends are now playing with the puppy?

One friend is quietly reading a book. One friend joins him or her and they begin to talk. How many friends are talking?

Nine friends arrive at the corner and look for the school bus. As they do not see the bus, three friends decide to walk to school. How many friends are still looking for the school bus?

Eight friends are practicing for a baseball game. One friend joins them. How many friends are practicing for the game?

Advancing Skill:

★ Solicit suggestions for dialogue from the children. What, for example, might the six friends playing baseball say to one another? Replay, changing the focus from pantomime to coordinated actions and dialogue.

Lifestyles of the Rich and Graphic

(Radio Spot)

Radio spots apply the concept of channel surfing to radio programs and provide amusing opportunities for vocal characterizations. For the script below, ask for volunteers to play the Talk Show Host, the Starlet, the Weather Forecaster, and the Teacher. Then, imagining that these characters are on four different radio programs, quickly change stations as the children read the lines in their character's voice. Cues should be picked up quickly. Amusement is found in whole sentences rather than in individual lines, so encourage a smooth flow from one character to the next. The rest of the class can have a copy of the script after the shows are "off the air," but they will have more fun listening than reading along as the programs are "broadcast."

Talk Show Host: Ladies and gentlemen, welcome to Celebrity Station where tonight our guests are . . .

Starlet: Paulette Picture Graph, the newest star in Graphywood. Of course, my picture on picture graphs always helps my fans to know . . .

Weather Forecaster: . . . if we will have rain. Looking at the bar graph of temperatures for the week, we can see that . . .

Talk Show Host: . . . ticket sales for your concerts reached a record high two years ago. This line graph, however, shows a decline after . . .

Weather Forecaster: . . . your updated travel forecast. We see on the bar graph that Detroit and Indianapolis . . .

Teacher: . . . had major changes in population. Census figures are plotted on this line graph which . . .

Starlet: . . . my agent has created. I use a pie graph to show the percentage of autographs I've signed for boys and for girls so that . . .

Weather Forecaster: . . . we can tell how our temperatures compare to this same week last year. Looking carefully at the bar graph, we . . .

Teacher: . . . notice that our population has changed. The line graph shows a decline in the number . . .

Talk Show Host: . . . of times our guest has appeared on our show. The audience will see that here is a picture graph of our celebrities. Your picture is on the graph four times. Your favorite dance partner appears on the graph three times. There are five pictures of . . .

Teacher: . . . various age groups. Using a pie graph, we can tell that most of the people in our state are between the ages of thirty and fifty–five. An almost equally high percentage are . . .

Talk Show Host: . . . appearing on our show next week.

Frankie the Fraction

(Noisy Story)

The math concepts of whole numbers and fractions are represented in this noisy story. Children form three groups and each group is matched to a character. The group playing Frankie the Fraction loudly practices his sound, "Part of a whole," before the teacher narrates the entire story. The groups playing Doris the Decimal and Harvey the Whole Number do likewise for their characters and sounds. When each group can loudly and confidently make their character's sound, the story is read aloud and the children add their sounds each time their character is mentioned.

After playing the story, it might be interesting to discuss the concept of "wholeness" with the children. In math, fractions combine to make a whole number. In terms of healthy self-concepts, however, do the children think that Frankie and Doris need each other to be "whole"? Why or why not?

> Frankie the Fraction — Part of a whole
> Doris the Decimal — Points, points
> Harvey the Whole Number — I'm a one!

Harvey the Whole Number* was a bully. "When are you going to grow up and be complete like me?" Harvey the Whole Number* smugly asked Frankie the Fraction*. "You've got parts missing," laughed Harvey the Whole Number* as he walked away from Frankie the Fraction*.

Frankie the Fraction* sat on a park bench and fought back tears. Frankie the Fraction* knew he was different but it hurt his feelings when Harvey the Whole Number* teased him about it. Everyone else in Frankie the Fraction's* class was complete, just like Harvey the Whole Number*, except for Doris the Decimal*. Doris the Decimal* was incomplete, too, but Frankie the Fraction* was too shy to talk to Doris the Decimal*.

Frankie the Fraction* stared at the ground. He didn't notice Doris the Decimal* coming toward the bench. When he heard Doris the Decimal* ask, "May I sit with you?" Frankie the Fraction* looked up and said, "Of course."

Doris the Decimal* sat next to Frankie the Fraction*. "I just saw Harvey the Whole Number*," she said. "Harvey the Whole Number* is such a bully! I hope he wasn't mean to you."

Frankie the Fraction* mustered his courage. "Sometimes," Frankie the Fraction* told Doris the Decimal*, "I think Harvey the Whole Number* is right. I don't feel complete."

Doris the Decimal* smiled. "Frankie the Fraction*," she said, "do you realize that you are a half and I am .50? Together, we make one. Together, we are the same as Harvey the Whole Number* and all of the other numbers in our class. When I feel sad about being incomplete, I think about all the friends that can join me to make me a whole. I am never lonely."

Frankie the Fraction* smiled. "I never thought of that," Frankie the Fraction* told Doris the Decimal*. "I'll remember and I'll never let Harvey the Whole Number* tease me again!"

Fraction Facts

(Concentration Game)

This variation of the *Addition and Subtraction Game* uses combinations for one fourth, one half, and one third. Before playing, we recommend that the teacher review these fraction combinations with the class so that the students are familiar with fractions that equal one half, one fourth, and one third.

Example:

Child 1: Two fourths equal one half.

Child 2: Two fourths equal one half. Six ninths equal two thirds.

Child 3: Two fourths equal one half. Six ninths equal two thirds. Two eighths equal one fourth.

My Watch

(Finger Play)

Wearing a watch can be a special treat for young people learning to tell time. This finger play helps kindergartners to recognize that a watch is a timekeeping instrument. After playing with the suggested motions, ask the children to make new actions for the poem.

My new watch has a leather band	(Strap on imaginary watch.)
Numbers on its face.	
It lets me know that I'm not late	(Smile!)
Racing place to place.	(Run in place.)
When both hands are at twelve o'clock	(Place both hands together at twelve o'clock position.)
Lunch is on my plate.	(Eat imaginary sandwich.)
It's time for me to go to sleep.	(Rest head on hands.)
The hour shown is eight.	(Place hands in eight o'clock position.)
I wear my watch to school each day.	(Look at imaginary watch on wrist.)
Minutes matter there.	(Lift wrist to ear and listen to watch ticking.)
My watch sits proudly on my wrist	(Pat top of wrist.)
Getting special care.	(Nod head up and down.)

Advancing Skill:

★ Using a model clock or felt board wrist watch, invite the children to set the hands to the appropriate times in the finger play.

Match the Time to the Action
(Pantomime)

Gr. 1-2

Engaging in unison play, the children pantomime an action appropriate to the time in the following sentences.

It's 7:00 A.M. and your alarm clock rings. What do you do?

It's 8:00 A.M. and you have to get ready for school. What do you do?

It's 9:00 A.M. and the teacher says it's time for reading. What do you do?

It's 10:00 A.M. and time for recess. What do you do?

It's noon and your stomach is growling. What do you do?

It's 3:00 P.M. and school buses are lined up in front of the building waiting to take children home. What do you do?

It's 4:00 P.M. and friends come to your house to play after school. What do you do?

It's 6:00 P.M. and Mom says it's time for dinner. What do you do?

It's 7:00 P.M. and Dad says you should do your homework. What do you do?

It's 9:00 P.M. and your parents say it's time to go to bed. What do you do?

Time Pantomimes
(Pantomime)

Gr. 3

The children assume the character of "Time" and pantomime the following. The activity lends itself well not only to the study of time but to a language arts exploration of how literal and figurative word use changes meanings.

1. Time flies
2. Time marches on

3. Time on one's hands
4. Father Time
5. Waste time
6. Once upon a time
7. A long time
8. Time's up
9. Spare time
10. In the nick of time
11. Make time
12. Take time

I Help in My Parents' Store
(Pantomime)

Several math concepts, including making change, are included in this story. Play it as a narrative pantomime with the exception that, when a math question is presented, children respond orally with the answer in addition to showing the appropriate action. Unison play affords all children the opportunity to play the main character. Ask them to think about who the "I" in the story might be. Is this a girl or boy? How old is the character? (Sidecoaching comments which the teacher may wish to make are included in parenthesis.)

My parents own a grocery store and I help them on Saturdays and after school.

Today, I have to stock a shelf. My dad wants me to put enough cans on the shelf so that a customer who has a dollar can buy all of them. Each can costs ten cents. How many cans should I put on the shelf? (I see some of you putting large cans on the shelf and others putting small cans on the shelf. What is in your cans?)

Next, I walk to the gumball machine. A little child is standing there, holding a quarter in her hand. She points to it. I show her the slot. "Put a nickel in there, turn the handle, and a gumball comes out." "Change, please," she says, and gives me her money. I reach into my pocket, pull out the coins, and count them. How many nickels should I give her? I give her change. "Show me, please," she says, so I take back a nickel, put it in the slot, and turn the handle. She takes the gumball and gleefully puts the candy in her mouth.

"Please help at the bottle return," I hear my Mother say, so I step behind the counter. A boy comes to the counter with four empty bottles. I must give him ten cents for each bottle he returns. I reach into the cash drawer. How much money should I give him? (What coins will you use?) He gives me the bottles and I give him the refund.

Mom needs help at the cash register so I walk to the front of the store. "Please check out this customer," Mom says. A man is buying some fruit. (What kind of fruit does the man have?) The total price is seventy-five cents. He hands me a dollar bill. How much change should I give him? I take the dollar, give him change, and put the fruit in a bag. I wave to him as he leaves the store.

Mom returns. "Thanks for helping," she says. "Because you have done such a good job today, I am giving you a tip." Mom hands me a quarter, two dimes, and a nickel. How much money do I have? I smile. "Thanks, Mom," I say, "I know just what I'll buy!" (Show what you will buy.)

A Year of Open-Ended Stories

(Story Creation)

Gr. K-3

The suggested grade levels for this story are deliberately broad. Young children might be expected to create only the briefest of stories but to really benefit from practice using the calendar. Older children will develop more elaborate stories but find calendar practice serving as review.

The teacher should introduce each story opening by asking the students to find that month on a calendar. We suggest playing the story for a particular month several times throughout that month in order to reinforce calendar use. Each time, a new plot should be developed from the opening provided. Stories can be completed orally or dramatized.

In January, Jasmine and Gerald are assigned a report on the life of Martin Luther King, Jr. "Let's go to the library," says Jasmine. "We can find books there about Dr. King," agrees Gerald. When they arrive at the library, the children . . .

In February, Jasmine and Gerald celebrate Valentine's Day by making valentines for their parents. "This year," says Jasmine, "let's surprise them. I have an idea," and she whispers in Gerald's ear. The children . . .

In March, Jasmine and Gerald read about St. Patrick and Ireland in school. "Let's look for four-leaf clovers after school," Jasmine tells Gerald. "I think they'll bring us luck and we'll meet a real leprechaun," thinks Gerald aloud. After school, the children . . .

In April, Jasmine and Gerald play in the puddles left by the spring rains. "I like to jump in the puddles and make a big splash," says Jasmine. "I can jump harder and higher than you," boasts Gerald. "Cannot," dares Jasmine. The children . . .

In May, Jasmine and Gerald go on a Memorial Day picnic. They pack a picnic basket and take the short walk to the park where they find a shady spot and spread their blanket. "Let's eat," declares Gerald. "Wait," whispers Jasmine, "we have a game to play first." The children . . .

In June, Jasmine and Gerald prepare for the end of the school year. They help the teacher put away books. They take special class trips and have special school events. On the last day of school, the children . . .

In July, Jasmine and Gerald go on vacation. Every year they visit a new place. They are very excited about their trip this year. "We're going someplace new," Jasmine excitedly announces. "Is it far away?" asks Gerald. "Further than you can imagine. We'll have to be brave when we get there, too," Jasmine answers. "What kind of place is this?" speaks Gerald softly. "I think we should prepare," announces Jasmine. The children . . .

In August, Jasmine and Gerald go shopping for new school clothes. "Now, I want you two to behave in the store," says Mother during the drive to the mall. Once inside the department store, however, the children . . .

In September, Jasmine and Gerald like to walk in the woods and collect leaves. One Saturday morning as they are hiking, the children . . .

In October, Jasmine and Gerald study Columbus' voyage in school. "Let's pretend that we are navigators," says Jasmine. "I hope we can discover new lands," wishes Gerald aloud. The children . . .

In November, Jasmine and Gerald celebrate Thanksgiving with their family. They travel to their Aunt Lucy's house for a feast and a visit with their aunt, uncle, and cousins. This year, on their way to Aunt Lucy's, the children . . .

In December, Jasmine and Gerald enjoy the first day of winter. They make snowmen, ice skate, or ski as a way of welcoming the season. "This year," says Jasmine, "let's do something different." Gerald smiles. "What should we do?" he asks. Jasmine and Gerald think silently for a moment. "I know! Come with me!" Jasmine shouts. The children . . .

Chapter 6

PHYSICAL EDUCATION

Content	Music/Creative Drama	
Coordination, Balance, Directionality, Following Directions	Movement:	Fundamental Patterns Bean Bag Circle the Bag Bag Out Nathan Visits the Park Under and Over the Moon Old Brass Wagon Paw Paw Patch Skip to My Lou Hop Old Squirrel
Fundamental Movements Done Creatively, Exercise Routines	Pantomime:	The Ball Workout Exercising with Mom The Relay Race
Independent Hand Coordination	Body Sounds:	Rondo Right and Left
Climbing	Pantomime:	CLIMB
Coordination	Song:	A Ram Sam Sam
Jumping Rope	Jump Rope Chant:	The Proposal Sailor My Bones
Sports Behavior	Pantomime:	Bad Sport/Good Sport

*M*any teachers are responsible for conducting physical education instruction within the school day. Integrating music and creative drama is a most natural activity in that movement is inherent in all three disciplines. This chapter spans rudimentary skills for primary children and develops fine motor skills and the physical education concepts of fair play and sports behavior.

Fundamental Patterns

(Movement)

Once children are familiar with fundamental movements, they can enjoy patterns of and variations on the basic moves. Create some simple sets of movements for routines. Give children minimal directions and use a small hand drum to provide a beat in a moderate tempo.

Examples:

drum: (4) ↓ | | | | ↓ | | | | ↓ | | | | ↓ | | | ‖

Point to right and walk in that direction for four beats.   ↓ | | | |

Point to left and walk in that direction for four beats.   ↓ | | | |

Point to sky and walk forward for four beats.   ↓ | | | |

Point to ground and walk backward for four beats.   ↓ | | | ‖

drum: (2)   ↓ | | ↓ | | ↓ | | ↓ | ‖

Hop on left foot.   ↓ | |

Hop on right foot.

Hop on left foot.

Clap and jump ¼ turn.

Repeat three more times until turns bring children facing forward.

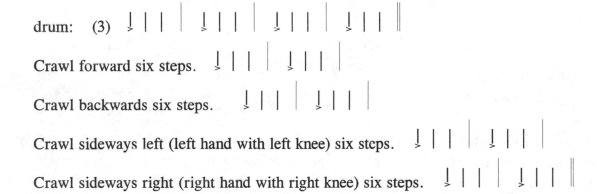

drum: (3)

Crawl forward six steps.

Crawl backwards six steps.

Crawl sideways left (left hand with left knee) six steps.

Crawl sideways right (right hand with right knee) six steps.

Each of the above fundamental patterns should bring the children back to their starting place.

Advancing Skill:

★ Initially the teacher may lead these routines by calling out the fundamental movements. From an inventory of movements listed on a chart, invite a child to select the movements and point to them at designated times.

Bean Bag
(Movement)

This warm-up game involves a partner and one bean bag between the two. With the partners facing each other and a short distance between them, ask the children to "hand over" the bag to one another on the beat. Ask the children to figure out what is the best hand to use in giving and receiving the bag. Allow them to experiment to find the most efficient and smooth movements.

Maintain the beat in different ways, such as playing a small hand drum; having the children chant rhymes, such as *Twinkle, Twinkle*; and having the children march in place.

As the children become more adept, have them practice tossing the bean bag to their partners. Again, note which hand tosses and which hand receives the bean bag.

Circle the Bag
(Movement)

With four or five children in a circle, provide one bean bag to each group. The object of the game is to toss the bag to the child on the right, keeping the bag moving on the beat. With a small hand drum, the leader starts the drum beat slowly and increases the speed so that passing becomes a coordination challenge. Remind the children that it is just as important to pass the bag as it is to receive the bag in time with the beat.

Bag Out
(Movement)

For this bag game, at least eight children should be seated in a circle on the floor. The goal is for the children to toss the bean bag to their right-hand neighbor on the beat while they recite chants.

If the bag comes to them during a "rest" (*i.e.*, a beat in which no words in the chant are voiced), they are "out." They should toss the bag to the person on their right before backing out of the circle. The circle tightens in size to accommodate lost players and continues until only one child remains.

Be sure to start with and maintain a steady beat in this game. Use familiar chants such as:

Peas Porridge Hot   *Five Little Monkeys*   *Hickory Dickory Dock*   *Bingo*

Nathan Visits the Park

(Movement)

Gr.
1-2

Pantomime sentences are an excellent way for children to participate in movement practice. By engaging in the same activities as Nathan, boys and girls get plenty of exercise. During this activity, children should have adequate space in which to move freely and safely.

Nathan likes to visit the park.

Nathan likes to glide quickly down the straight slide when he visits the park.

Nathan likes to duck in and out of the bars on the jungle gym when he visits the park.

Nathan likes to soar high above the ground on the swings when he visits the park.

Nathan likes to try to throw his ball into the basket on the basketball court when he visits the park.

Nathan likes to eat his lunch at a picnic table when he visits the park.

Nathan likes to buy chocolate ice cream from the vendor when he visits the park.

Nathan likes to throw and catch a Frisbee when he visits the park.

Nathan likes to bounce up and down on the teeter totter when he visits the park.

Nathan likes to ride on the spring ponies when he visits the park.

Nathan likes to climb on all of the climbing toys when he visits the park.

Nathan likes to crawl through the tall grass when he visits the park.

Nathan likes to jump over the hurdles when he visits the park.

Nathan likes to twist and turn as he moves down the curved slide when he visits the park.

Nathan likes to walk up and down the rope ladder when he visits the park.

Nathan likes to swing on the long rope that reminds him of a monkey vine when he visits the park.

Nathan likes to rest under the big shady tree when he visits the park.

Advancing Skill:

★ With the children, select other sites Nathan might visit and determine the movement activities that might occur there. As a group, pantomime these movements.

Under and Over the Moon
(Movement)

Using a long jump rope, ask the children to practice basic movements such as walking, gliding, and galloping as they come under the jump rope and over it. Hold the jump rope about three feet off the ground for "under" movements. The object is to avoid touching the jump rope. Encourage students to walk, jump, and slide in creative ways. Pretend the rope is a big heavy cloud or a low ceiling in an attic.

Review the same movements with the jump rope about six inches off the ground for the "over" movements. Pretend the rope is a big alligator or an ice cold wave. While the children take turns, ask them to observe the movements of their classmates and note the creativity.

Old Brass Wagon
(Movement)

Some "oldies but goodies" in the genre of American folk dances have earned their place in history for a good reason: they are fun! Just as you would expose children to important American folk songs and literature, introduce them to folk dances. Though some dances are best performed with recorded music, *Old Brass Wagon* has directions built into its lyrics, so we recommend that you teach the song first:

1.Cir-cle to the left, old brass wag-on, Cir-cle to the left, old brass wag-on,

Cir-cle to the left, old brass wag-on, You're the one, my dar - lin'!

Additional Verses:

2.   Circle to the right, old brass wagon, Circle to the right, old brass wagon,
     Circle to the right, old brass wagon, You're the one, my darlin'!

3.   Swing, oh, swing, old brass wagon, Swing, oh, swing, old brass wagon,
     Swing, oh, swing, old brass wagon, You're the one, my darlin'!

4.   Skipping all around, old brass wagon, Skipping all around, old brass wagon,
     Skipping all around, old brass wagon, You're the one, my darlin'!

Directions:

Make a circle with each girl alternating with a boy.

Verse 1:   Circle left.

Verse 2:   Circle right.

Verse 3:   Partners face each other, hold hands and swing around once on each "swing, oh, swing" phrase.

Verse 4:   Girls stand on boys' right, making an inner circle. Partners link elbows and skip clockwise around the circle.

This song helps reinforce directionality, clockwise and counterclockwise motion.

Paw Paw Patch

(Movement)

Gr.
1-2

This folk song involves a simple line dance—actually a two–line dance. The directions are suggested by the lyrics, so learn the song before engaging the children in the dance.

Where, oh, where is pret-ty lit-tle Su-sie,   Where, Oh, Where is pret-ty lit-tle Su-sie?

Where, oh, where is pret-ty lit-tle Su-sie,   Way down yon-der in the paw paw patch.

Additional Verses:

2. Come on, boys, let's go find her,
    Come on, boys, let's go find her,
    Come on, boys, let's go find her,
    Way down yonder in the paw paw patch.

3. Pickin' up paw paws, put 'em in your pocket,
    Pickin' up paw paws, put 'em in your pocket,
    Pickin' up paw paws, put 'em in your pocket,
    Way down yonder in the paw paw patch.

Directions:

Form two lines—girls in one, boys in the other, girls facing boys.

Verse 1:   The first girl skips a circle around both lines and returns to her place.

Verse 2:   The first girl repeats her skipping with the entire line of boys following her. They return to their original positions.

Verse 3:   The first girl and the first boy skip to the back of their lines (with the rest of the children following). They form an arch and the rest of the children "pick up paw paws" as they go through the arch.

Skip to My Lou

(Movement)

Not all children can skip, but this song may encourage everyone to try. Once the song is learned, children can stand in a circle to sing and act out the motions of the first three phrases. On the words, "Skip to my Lou, my darling," they can skip.

1. Flies in the butter-milk, shoo, shoo, shoo! Flies in the butter-milk, shoo, shoo, shoo!
Flies in the butter-milk, shoo, shoo, shoo! Skip to my Lou, my dar - ling.

Additional Verses:

2. Little red wagon, painted blue,
   Little red wagon, painted blue,
   Little red wagon, painted blue,
   Skip to my Lou, my darling.

3. Lost my partner, what'll I do?
   Lost my partner, what'll I do?
   Lost my partner, what'll I do?
   Skip to my Lou, my darling.

4. I'll find another one prettier than you.
   I'll find another one prettier than you.
   I'll find another one prettier than you.
   Skip to my Lou, my darling.

5. Hurry up, slow poke, do, oh, do.
   Hurry up, slow poke, do, oh, do.
   Hurry up, slow poke, do, oh, do.
   Skip to my Lou, my darling.

6. One old boat and a run down shoe.
   One old boat and a run down shoe.
   One old boat and a run down shoe.
   Skip to my Lou, my darling.

7. Kitten in the hay mow, mew, mew, mew.
   Kitten in the hay mow, mew, mew, mew.
   Kitten in the hay mow, mew, mew, mew.
   Skip to my Lou, my darling.

Advancing Skill:

★ In addition to singing with movements, this skill develops the children's inner hearing by asking them to hear the song inside of them. During the song, motion "ssh" (index finger over your lips) as a sign for the song to continue in the children's heads. To illustrate:

Sing phrases 1 and 2.

"Ssh" phrase 3. (Movements continue.)

Remove "ssh" sign and resume to sing phrase 4.

Encourage children to keep the song going (not rushing or slowing the tempo) inside of their heads as they continue the motions.

Allow children to lead the "ssh" game.

Hop Old Squirrel
(Movement)

In this little dance-song from Germany, the movements are prescribed. Not all kindergartners will be able to hop, however, this song may encourage careful balance and practice.

Hop, old squirrel, ei-dle-dum, ei-dle-dum, Hop, old squirrel, ei-dle-dum, dee!

Hop, old squirrel, ei-dle-dum, ei-dle-dum, Hop, old squirrel, ei-dle-dum,-dee!

Ask each child to think of new movements for the squirrel, such as stoop, reach, and twist. Perform the varied motions.

The Ball

(Pantomime)

Children can demonstrate both fine and gross motor skills when playing with balls. The verbs in this activity describe actions which can be successfully demonstrated using movements. As the poem is narrated, children communicate many different ways of handling this versatile and familiar orb.

Pass it.
Dribble it.
Dunk it.

Kick it.
Roll it.
Bounce it.

Pitch it.
Hit it.
Catch it.

Pass it.
Toss it.
Bowl it.

There are so many things
To do with a ball.

Workout

(Pantomime)

Children see fundamental movements when they watch workouts on exercise videos and television programs. They will need to have plenty of room for this narrative poem in which fitness and fun are paired.

Stretch so high.
Bend so low.
This exercise is fun.
Touch my toes.
Swing my arms.
My workout's just begun.

Jumping jacks,
Jumping jacks,
How many can I do?
Run in place.
Run in place.
I'll run along with you.

Pushups now,
I'll do ten.
I certainly am strong!
Muscles firm,
Look at me
Sweating to a song.

I've stretched high.
I've bent low.
My workout now is done.
Cooling down,
Cooling down,
This exercise is fun!

Exercising with Mom

(Pantomime)

This activity serves the same purpose as *Workout*, but is designed for older children. Play this in pairs, with one student as Mom and the other as the child in the story.

Every morning before she gets ready for work, Mom plays a workout tape on the VCR. I like to exercise with her.

First, we spread our mats on the floor. Mom has one and so do I. The tape begins. We stand with our feet apart and swing our arms from right to left. We twist from side to side.

We bend at the waist. We try to touch our elbows to our knees. We touch our right elbow to our left knee and then our left elbow to our right knee. We do this several times. We stand up straight again and twist. This time, we keep our elbows close to our bodies. Mom says this is easier if we keep the palms of our hands up and keep our elbows close to our waists. I try to look just like Mom as she does this.

Next, we get down on our mats. We do sit ups. These are easy, but the next part is hard. Now, we have to lift our legs and keep them straight and then we have to reach our arms back and forth to our knees. Mom doesn't like this exercise. Next, we keep our legs straight up and touch our elbows to our knees. This is a little easier.

I like rocking back and forth on my hips. Mom smiles whenever she sees me do the hip rocker. After that, I put my legs together and push out and back. I can do this many times. So can Mom.

We're almost finished as we hug our knees to our chests. "Press hard," says the lady on the tape and we do. Now, we can relax!

Advancing Skills:

★What other physical fitness activities do the children enjoy doing with an adult? Invite the children to identify the fundamental movements inherent in these and to create pantomimes for their choices, using *Exercising with Mom* as a model.

★ Replay the above with movements from activities which might be done in the home. What fundamental movements, for example, are inherent in cleaning the house or cooking a meal?

The Relay Race
(Pantomime)

Initially, play the poem as a narrative pantomime with all of the children moving as each of the characters.

Last night I had the strangest dream
About a relay race.
A snail was captain of our team.
He set a sluggish pace.

A bunny was the next in line.
He hopped from end to end.
A snake then slithered up and back.
He was the bunny's friend.

"Faster," I cried. "We must gain speed."
The elephant was next.
His trunk he swung from side to side.
The other team looked vexed.

"I'll pounce," said panther, full of pride,
"I am an agile cat."
We all admired his graceful stride
And wished we moved like that.

A deer came leaping after him.
A bug next crawled so quickly
I told my team, "Hope's not so dim."
The other team looked sickly.

So I prepared to run the course.
I knew I had to try
To win the race. "Good luck," stamped horse.
My feet were going to fly.

When back to horse I ran at last
I knew we were ahead.
But I don't know who won the race
'Cause I fell out of bed.

Advancing Skills:

★ Play the poem a second time and cast both "teams." Who is on the other team? Are there animals? How do they move?

★ Ask the children to add dialogue, cheering, *etc.*, when you play the poem.

★ Play the race in slow motion.

★ Select several children to be a broadcast team and announce the progress of the race for an imaginary television audience.

★ Have a relay race with the children first in teams comprised of animals. Replay with the children in human teams. Compare the movements used.

Rondo Right and Left

(Body Sounds)

The coordination goal in this activity is for the children to execute one musical line without being distracted by another. Try the following rondo with half of the children using their right hands and the other half using their left hands for the first four measures. Upon the repeat sign, the children change hand parts—right handers now performing the left-hand part and vice versa.

Part A (3)   Right Hand
              Left Hand Patschen
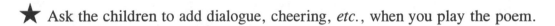
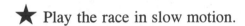

Part B   RH

          LH

Part A   RH

          LH

Part C   RH

          LH

Part A   RH

          LH

:‖   =   Repeat sign

CLIMB
(Pantomime)

Children play the following sentences in pantomime. After playing, ask them to identify different ways in which they climbed. They may want to demonstrate their answers.

C   You are a **chimpanzee climbing** up a tree and swinging on the branches.

L   You are a **letter carrier climbing** a flight of stairs in an apartment building and delivering a letter.

I   You are **ivy climbing** up a trellis.

M   You are a **mountain climber climbing** up the side of a steep cliff.

B   You are a hot air **balloon climbing** from the ground and floating high in the sky.

Advancing Skill:

★ Ask for other people and things that could fit into the sequence. Replay with the new items.

A Ram Sam Sam

(Song)

These nonsense words fit the nonsense motions below. Be sure to rehearse the song well before trying it as a round. The coordination of movements during the round performance may prove distracting, but encourage children to maintain their part.

Directions:

1. For each "**ram sam sam**," patsch, clap clap.

2. On "**guli guli guli guli guli**," roll hands around one another. Repeat #1 for "**ram sam sam.**"

3. During "**a rafi**," cup right elbow with left hand and trace a circular motion with right hand. Repeat with second "**a rafi**," using other hand and arm.

4. Repeat same actions for "**guli**" and "**ram sam sam**."

Advancing Skills:

★ Choreograph another set of movements which fit the structure of the song.

★ Clap the round based on the rhythms.

★ Trace the contour of the melody (upward and downward motion) with hands.

The Proposal
(Jump Rope Chant)

Options for playing this jump rope chant make it a versatile activity. Learning the words is suggested before the boys and girls select any of the following.

1. Pantomime the chant individually, playing both characters. Then jump rope while counting the miles that Johnny walks.

2. Select a partner and pantomime the chant with one person as Johnny and the other as the young lady. Next, ask two classmates to turn the rope. All four participants count the miles.

The Proposal

Johnny brought me flowers,
Got down on one knee.
"You are such a special girl.
Will you marry me?"

I took Johnny's flowers,
Tossed the gift aside.
"No. I cannot marry you.
I won't be your bride."

"Then I'll find another,
One who will be true.
I will walk a million miles
To get away from you."

One, two, three, *etc.* (Count each jump as a mile that Johnny walks.)

Sailor

(Jump Rope Chant)

Each of the following rhymes ends with counting the number of jumps a child successfully completes.

Sailor should be played first as a finger play and then as a jump rope chant.

I am a sailor as you see.	(point thumbs to chest with pride)
I sail the ocean happily.	(hand to forehead as if looking at sea)
I count the waves the whole day through	(count fingers)
And now I'd like to count with you.	(point to your neighbor)

One, two, *etc.*

My Bones

(Jump Rope Chant)

Working on mats, the children pantomime climbing, falling, popping, dangling, and tumbling when learning the following rhyme.

I climb the stairs to the attic.
I climb the stairs to the top.
If I fall backwards down the stairs
My bones will surely pop!

How many bones would tumble fast?
How many dangle freely?
You'd have to count the bones for me.
I'd need your help then, really!

One, two, *etc.*

Bad Sport/Good Sport

(Pantomime)

Working in pairs and using pantomime, one player shows Barney's actions and the other shows Gracie's. After playing the poem once, switch roles and replay.

Barney is a bad sport.
He cheats at games he plays.
If he can't win, he pouts and sulks
And takes the ball away.

Gracie is a good sport
And when the game is through,
She always shakes her rival's hand.
She knows it's polite to do.

Barney cries, yells, and screams
If things don't go his way.
He calls his rivals nasty names,
Ignores rules of fair play.

Gracie doesn't argue,
Accepts officials' calls.
Win, lose, or draw, when Gracie plays
She says, "Good job!" to all.

Barney picks as teammates
Players who are aces.
"No losers here," he firmly vows,
Making ugly faces.

Gracie's team really tries
Giving each child a turn.
"When all can play, the game's more fun,"
Says Gracie with concern.

Good sportsmanship's a goal
In every game we play.
Let's make our motto, "Fair, fun, fair!"
And practice it each day.

Advancing Skills:

★ Solicit other examples of good and bad sportsmanship from the students and ask that these be included in a new poem that the class creates and then pantomimes.

★ Working in small groups, children can identify examples of good sportsmanship and fair play that they have witnessed at recess, in gym class, at sporting events and elsewhere. Each group should create pantomime sentences which illustrate these behaviors. The groups can then trade their lists with each other and pantomime the sentences. The activity can be replayed with examples of poor sportsmanship.

★With the children seated in a circle, the teacher begins a concentration game by naming a behavior that demonstrates good sportsmanship. The child to his or her left repeats the phrase and the teacher's item, and then adds a new behavior. The game continues in this manner, with each person repeating the phrase, the actions already named, and then adding an example of good sportsmanship or fair play.

Teacher: I am going to help Barney learn to be a good sport. I will teach him to wait his turn.

Child 1:   I am going to help Barney learn to be a good sport. I will teach him to wait his turn and to shake his opponent's hand.

Child 2:   I am going to help Barney learn to be a good sport. I will teach him to wait his turn, to shake his opponent's hand, and to put away the equipment he uses.

Chapter 7

SCIENCE

Content	Music/Creative Drama	
Animal Kingdom	Name Game:	Animal Life
	Chant:	Itsy Bitsy Spider
	Song:	Mulberry Bush
	Creative Movement:	Animal Antics
	Pantomime:	Di-no Di-no Dinosaur
	Body Sculptures:	Dinosaur
	Story Dramatization:	A Dog's Life
Senses	Finger Play:	Your Senses
Environmental Awareness	Finger Play:	Reuse, Recycle
Planets	Name Game:	Planets
	Pantomime:	Exploring the Planets
	Story Creation:	A Space Adventure
Construction	Song:	Wise Man Built His House upon the Rock
Magnets	Creative Movement:	Magnetic Motion
Electricity	Pantomime:	Zeke Gets Zapped
	Sequence Game:	Ben Franklin Experiments with Electricity
Elements of Weather	Name Game:	Elements of Weather
	Body Sounds:	Rainstorm
Seasons	Finger Play:	Swimming Pool
	Creative Movement:	The Snow Is Dancing
	Pantomime:	Season Sights
Stars and Direction (North, South, East, West)	Pantomime:	Time, Place, Action Maui Nooses the Sun
Inventions	Characterization:	Interviewing Inventors
States of Matter	Quieting Activities:	Rain, Snow

*S*cience units are multifaceted. The content may cover such topics as animal and plant life, the environment, elements of weather or intergalactic activities.

Keen observation and a curiosity for why things work the way they do are two strategies fostered in this chapter. Music and creative drama can assist children's absorption and enjoyment of science.

Animal Life

(Name Game)

Make name tags in the shape of animals. Place children's names on tags. These tags can be used and reused for a variety of activities in this chapter. Consider integrating animal name tags with the following songs:

1. *Farmer in the Dell*
2. *Old MacDonald Had a Farm*
3. *Mary Had a Little Lamb* (or dog, cow, pig)
4. *Hop Old Squirrel*
5. *Bingo*

Advancing Skill:

★ Ask children to classify animals on name tags. For example, animals that live in water, animals that have legs, animals that can fly, *etc*.

Itsy Bitsy Spider

(Chant)

What can we learn about spiders from this familiar finger play? It is also useful for improving fine motor skills. Teach the children the words, giving the chant a sense of rhythmic motion:

Itsy bitsy spider went up the water spout.
Down came the rain and washed the spider out.
Out came the sun and dried up all the rain.
Itsy bitsy spider climbed up the spout again.

Model the following hand movements:

Line 1: Press left thumb and right index finger together. Press left index finger and right thumb together. Repeat by "walking" the finger movements upward.

Line 2: Wiggle fingers downward and wash away the rain.

Line 3: Open arms, making an arch to the left with the left arm, one to the right with the right arm.

Line 4: Repeat motions as in line 1.

Combine chant with motions when words and movements are secure.

Advancing Skills:

★ Change the speed of the chant and movements for an energetic, physically fit spider and a lazy, tired spider.

★ Discuss why spiders might be climbing up a water spout. After your discussion, make up a story as to why the itsy bitsy spider wants to climb up there.

★ Look at spiders or pictures of them. Notice the number of legs. Compare and contrast them with other insects. Classify them as insect species. Discuss behaviors of insects.

Mulberry Bush

(Song)

Teach the **Mulberry Bush** with the suggested movements. It will form a basis for variations involving animals and typical movements.

1. Here we go 'round the mul-ber-ry bush, the mul-ber-ry bush, the mul-ber-ry bush.

Here we go 'round the mul-ber-ry bush, so ear-ly in the morn - ing.

Advancing Skill:

★ Using animal name tags (from **Animal Life**), substitute the names of animals that invite characteristic movement. For example:

This is the way a pony trots . . .
This is the way an elephant tromps . . .
This is the way an alligator crawls . . .
This is the way a kangaroo jumps . . .

Animal Antics

(Creative Movement)

While children in kindergarten through second grade will enjoy characterizing animals in the previous activity, third graders will be challenged by this more sophisticated creative movement opportunity. Each of these following terms is used to describe a group of animals. Children should apply the literal meaning to the word group and demonstrate it in pantomime. Our students, for example, have used "school of fish" to show fish boarding a bus, arriving at the classroom, learning lessons, taking tests, and reading books.

School of fish   Team of horses
Flock of sheep   Herd of cattle
Pack of wolves   Gaggle of geese
Skulk of foxes

Di-no Di-no Dinosaur

(Pantomime)

Children always enjoy learning about dinosaurs. In this poem, they have an opportunity to characterize these giant beasts. Before playing, discuss the size and weight of dinosaurs that would shake and quake the earth. Ask the children to envision and try on animals as large as the room.

Di-no, Di-no, Dinosaur
Tromping, stomping
Hear him roar.

Moving, moving Dinosaur
Shaking, quaking
Earth's deep core.

Mighty, mighty Dinosaur
Pounding, bounding
Conqueror.

Ancient, ancient Dinosaur
Gone forever
Rules no more.

Dinosaur
(Body Sculptures)

For second and third graders, pantomiming Di-no can serve as a warm-up for dinosaur body sculptures. Students can move from creating body sculptures based upon dinosaurs they have studied to creating new species which they invent and name from imagination.

A Dog's Life
(Story Dramatization)

Creative movements can be applied to this contrasting study of a young puppy and her older friend. In preparation for playing, those children who have dogs might describe how the animal moves, if their pet is a puppy or older, and tricks it might know. After several students have volunteered information about their pets, solicit a comparison of movements for other young and older animals.

Be sure the students try on both Flip and Spot in preparation for the story dramatization.

Flip loved her home. The active puppy had lots of new places to explore and a family that adored her. "This is great!" thought Flip, as she nibbled at her puppy food. Flip shared the house with Spot, an older dog who had been with the family a long time. Spot often watched Flip scampering around the house. "I must teach Spot to play with me!" Flip decided.

Flip bounded over to Spot as the older dog was eating her breakfast. "Let's race," said the puppy. She sped across the room. Spot walked slowly to Flip. "I can't move as quickly as you do, Flip. I am not as young," she said gently.

"Watch me do tricks," said Flip. "I can roll over. I can beg. Can you?" Flip rolled over three times and then raised herself up on her hind paws and held out her front paws. Spot rolled over once. She rolled over slowly. She begged. Flip was surprised to see how much bigger Spot was when the older dog raised her paws. "Will I ever be as big as you are?" she asked. "Of course," said Spot.

"Now, I'll teach you a trick," Spot told Flip. "When you meet someone new, hold out your paw and shake hands." She showed the puppy what to do. "You try it," she said. Flip held out her paw, but decided that a hug would be better. She leapt at her playmate and tried to embrace her. Spot moved out of the way and reminded Flip to be careful. "You could knock someone down, Flip. If you're happy to see someone, wag your tail," and she swished her tail from side to side. Flip thought that looked like fun and quickly beat the air with her tail.

Spot yawned. "It's time for my nap now, Flip." She circled the carpet once and then rested on her stomach. She closed her eyes. "I want to be like Spot when I get bigger," Flip decided, and she circled the carpet once, rested on her stomach, and closed her eyes. She dreamt of playing happily with Spot for many days to come.

Advancing Skill:

★ Replay the story with two new animals, one young and one older. With the children, select new characters and determine how they might move. How will their movements contrast? Adapt the story accordingly before replaying.

Your Senses

(Finger Play)

Gr. K-1

The children should point to each body part as it's mentioned in the finger play. Participation will help young learners connect sensory function to body part.

You have a nose for smelling	(Point to nose.)
Both odors sweet and foul.	(Sniff.)
And ears are there for hearing	(Point to ear.)
A whisper or a growl.	(Cup hand to ear.)

Your tongue can tell the diff'rence	(Point to tongue.)
'Tween spicy food and bland.	(Lick lips.)
And touching is a job for	(Touch one hand with the other.)
The fingers on your hand.	(Wiggle fingers.)
You have two eyes for seeing	(Point to eyes.)
What goes on around you.	(Look from side to side.)
Your senses are good helpers	(Make "okay" sign with fingers.)
In everything you do.	(Move "okay" sign back and forth.)

Advancing Skill:

★ Ask for suggestions for other sensory connections. What else, for example, might noses smell? Invite the children to pantomime these new suggestions, pointing first to the appropriate body part and then demonstrating the function.

Reuse, Recycle

(Finger Play)

Gr. K-1

This finger play can be used to reinforce the importance of taking care of the earth. After playing, ask the children to identify items they can recycle. They might also construct a collage using pictures of recycled products.

Reuse, recycle, don't abuse.	(Wag finger in admonition.)
We've got to save the planet.	(Draw large round circle in the air with index finger.)
The fire of pollution burns too bright	(Wiggle fingers in the air like dancing flames.)
And we don't need to fan it.	(Fan the air.)

Advancing Skill:

★ Question the children about recycled products they might use in their homes. While young children are unlikely to have extensive knowledge about them, most will be aware of common things like soda pop cans. Request that they pantomime using each of these products before it is recycled.

Planets
(Name Game)

In this project, the children learn characteristics of the planets—their relative size, composition, likely coloring, and so forth. The children select a planet of their choice and construct it out of poster board and yarn. The characteristics of the planet are to be sewn with yarn on the planet, *e.g.*, surface texture, rings, or coloring. The children introduce themselves and their planets by sharing the reason why they selected their planet and special characteristics that they've constructed.

Variation:

Match the rhythm of the planet's name to the child's name. For example:

Jupiter = Marilynn
Venus = Stephen
Mars = Tom

Exploring the Planets
(Pantomime)

Children enjoy space adventures, and this narrative pantomime story takes them on a journey through the solar system. Introduce the story by casting all of the students as astronauts of the future. Set the scene by telling them that their space travel occurs at a time when scientific advances have made it possible to explore previously prohibitive environments. Their explorations make them pioneers in planetary investigation.

You are an astronaut and your mission is to explore the planets. As you encounter each one, your actions are being recorded by an on-board camera and sent back to Earth, so be certain that your movements show what you are seeing and feeling.

The first stop is Mercury. As you step onto the planet, you are surprised by how dry, airless, and silent it seems. As you move about, you notice that there are craters separated by smooth plains. You are glad that you are physically fit as you walk over some of the lumpy hills. Some of these hills are over a mile high and you feel like it takes a long time to climb them. The day that you spend on Mercury is very hot, but the night is very cold. You are glad to return to your ship.

Your next stop is Venus. The lightning and rain that you saw as you descended never reach the surface of the planet. You inspect your protective clothing before leaving your ship because sulfuric acid from the yellowish clouds could burn human skin. Once you are outside of the vehicle, you squint but it does no good. You notice that nothing that is more than a hundred yards away can be seen clearly. You move cautiously and with difficulty because of crushing atmospheric pressure. From Earth, Venus is the brightest planet in the night sky. Now that you are standing on the planet, you must inspect the constantly erupting volcanoes and the red glow of the rocks. As you investigate each part of the planet, you find mountains, canyons, and plateaus. You look up into Venus' red sky but you cannot find a moon.

You return to the ship and head for Mars. When you arrive at the red planet and begin to search the terrain, you have to maneuver over a rocky surface. It is hard to see because there is so much dust. It is easy to walk because gravity here is weaker than it is on Earth. You jump. On Earth, you notice, that jump would put you about three feet into the air but here it propels you eight and a half feet. You check your protective clothing because on Mars, without it, your blood could boil. Assured that you are safe, you move on until you find a giant canyon. It's really big! You also discover, as you move around the planet, that there are two polar ice caps, volcanoes, and craters. When you return to the ship, you eat a big dinner. After all, although you weigh one hundred pounds on Earth, you weigh only thirty-eight pounds on Mars, so you can eat a lot.

Now it's on to the biggest planet, Jupiter. Before landing, you count fifteen moons and a narrow ring as you orbit the planet. You record these sightings in your journal. On Jupiter, you see colored clouds and grand auroras brightening the polar sky. As you exit the ship and begin to move about, you notice it is hard to walk because Jupiter has strong gravity. You want to explore the Giant Red Spot as it changes from red to full brick red, so you set up some special equipment that will send pictures back to Earth for later use.

You return to your ship and set a course for a flight that will take you past Saturn, Uranus, Neptune, and Pluto. Lean back in your chair as the ship speeds through space. Close your eyes and rest.

You awaken to the sight of big rings. Draw these in your journal. You are passing Saturn. As you fly near the surface of the planet, you look out the window at cream- and beige-colored clouds. One cloud is shaped like a six. Trace its shape with your finger. Notice how big this cloud is. Take a map of the United States from storage and draw a line between Los Angeles and New York. That is how big this cloud is!

As you fly into the solar sky, you pass Uranus and Neptune. Both are a greenish color. Find a green marker and some paper among your recording devices. Draw both planets and color them with the marker. Use the marker to write the names of the planets on the drawing. Tuck the paper neatly inside your journal. You will want to keep this drawing with your other personal records.

Now you turn to the camera that is sending pictures of your trip to Earth and make a small circle with your hands. You want people watching to know that you have just passed the small planet of Pluto.

Now your ship turns in space and you head for home. Take your seat on the flight deck and turn on a monitor. Immediately, a picture of a planet that is shaped like a ball and covered by oceans appears. Earth! You will soon be home. Lean back in your seat and smile.

A Space Adventure

(Story Creation)

All planets in the solar system can eventually be explored through the adventure stories of Cara and Carl, two young space pioneers. Use the following opening and invite the children to create orally or through dramatization the rest of the story. Simply changing "first stop" to "next stop" facilitates additional adventures during replay.

"Three, two, one, lift-off!" Cara closed her eyes and Carl whispered, "Wow," as the rocket climbed off the pad and soared into space. They could hardly believe that the adventure had really begun.

Cara and Carl were the first children trained as astronauts and their mission was to travel from Earth to the planets and to colonize each so that children could safely live there. The first stop would be . . .

Advancing Skills:

★ You may also wish to add music to the stories. Allow children to create an introduction or overture for the story, sound effects, *etc.*

★ Listen to *The Planets* by Holst for an aural experience which would blend well with this activity. You also could play this as the children are creating their space adventures.

★ Divide the class into nine groups and assign each group one planet. Group members then determine characters, a problem or conflict encountered on that planet, and a solution. Give each group time to create, rehearse, and dramatize its story of planet exploration. Have members share their finished work with the other groups. During replay, groups can exchange planets and determine new characters, conflicts, and solutions.

Wise Man Built His House upon the Rock
(Song)

Have you ever built a sandcastle? Why is it fun to make castles with sand? Have you ever built an ice fort? Why is it fun to make forts with ice? Will a sandcastle or ice fort last a long time? Why or why not? This song explores building foundations.

Teach this song with the movements suggested:

Oh the wise man built his house up-on the rock, Oh the

wise man built his house up-on the rock, Oh the wise man built his

house up-on the rock and the rains came tumb-ling down.

Additional Verses:

2. Oh the rains came down and the floods came up,
    Oh the rains came down and the floods came up,
    Oh the rains came down and the floods came up,
    But the house on the rock stood firm.

3. Oh the silly man built his house upon the sand,
    Oh the silly man built his house upon the sand,
    Oh the silly man built his house upon the sand,
    And the rains came tumbling down.

4. Oh the rains came down and the floods came up,
    Oh the rains came down and the floods came up,
    Oh the rains came down and the floods came up,
    And the house on the sand went swisssssssssssh.

Directions:

"wise man"   (Point to brain.)

"built"   (Bop hands.)

"house"   (Make peaked roof with hands.)

"rock"   (Show flat, solid line.)

"foolish man"	(Point circular motion to brain.)
"sand"	(Show wavy motion.)
"rain"	(Wiggle fingers downward.)
"floods"	(Raise hands upward.)

Advancing Skills:

★ Play the Japanese game of rock, paper, and scissors with hand motions. Discuss qualities of natural materials such as stone, paper (wood), and metal.

★ Where do you find houses built on sand? Why isn't it smart?

Magnetic Motion
(Creative Movement)

Children are fascinated by the properties of magnets, that is, their weight and attraction and repulsion characteristics. They can demonstrate their understanding of these properties by moving accordingly.

Designate a number of students to behave as magnets with their right sides being the "positives" and left sides being "negatives." As they move about, check to see that points of clinging or separation are correct. To inspire movements, play recordings of relatively slow, new age jazz.

Zeke Gets Zapped
(Pantomime)

All of the children should play Zeke in this narrative pantomime poem. The last line of each verse, however, should be spoken by the children in unison.

A tale of woe about poor Zeke
It is my task to tell.
He touched a light switch with wet hands.
We all could hear him yell.
Zeke gets zapped!

A storm came up and poor old Zeke
Sought shelter 'neath a tree.
When lightning knocked him to the ground,
He was a sight to see.
Zeke gets zapped!

The television Zeke did watch
While bathing in his tub,
Fell in and gave him quite a shock.
He had no time to scrub.
Zeke gets zapped!

Zeke tried to fix the radio
But let the music play.
Now Zeke hears songs that are not there,
But can't tell what *we* say.
Zeke gets zapped!

A wire underneath the rug
Zeke thought that he could hide.
A fire burned the carpeting,
And Zeke just cried and cried.
Zeke gets zapped!

Zeke used a socket that was full,
Circuits overloaded.
There was a short, sharp crackling sound,
Light bulbs then exploded.
Zeke gets zapped!

A cable on the ground Zeke saw,
Wanted to retrieve it.
The current made him jerk so much
We could not believe it.
Zeke gets zapped!

Electrifying though they are,
Zeke's feats you shouldn't try.
Take care with wires and with plugs
Or you, like Zeke, will fly.
Don't get zapped!

Ben Franklin Experiments with Electricity

(Sequence Game)

Our students enjoy "reading" the physical actions of their classmates as well as reading their cards when playing sequence games. They watch closely to see if the actions being performed match those that constitute their cue. As a warm-up for these games, we suggest mirroring activities, where boys and girls try to replicate precisely the movements and actions of partners. These help prepare for the careful watching needed to recognize when it is their turn in this more complex progression activity.

The following sequence game combines the study of an historical figure, characterization, and science. When playing, each student assumes the role of Benjamin Franklin.

> You start the game. Come to the center of the room and pantomime meeting Dr. Spence from Scotland, talking with him about electricity, and buying his machine that gives out electric sparks.

The person before you pantomimed meeting Dr. Spence from Scotland, talking with him about electricity, and buying his machine that gives out electric sparks.

You come to the center of the room and pantomime showing someone that your new machine is a glass tube with a crank, cranking the device, and then touching the person and shocking him or her.

The person before you pantomimed showing someone that your new machine is a glass tube with a crank, cranking the device, and then touching the person and shocking him or her.

You come to the center of the room and pantomime making the first electric battery using pieces of window glass and metal.

The person before you pantomimed making the first electric battery using pieces of window glass and metal.

You come to the center of the room and pantomime building machines that give off sparks and then testing how electricity acts on various objects. As you experiment, show if the objects are wet or dry, what they are made of, and their temperature.

The person before you pantomimed building machines that give off sparks and then testing how electricity acts on various objects. As the person experimented, he or she showed if the objects were wet or dry, what they were made of, and their temperature.

You come to the center of the room, show that you are proud of your successful experiments producing electrical sparks, pantomime boasting to your friends that you are going to use electricity to kill a turkey, and show them how tender and delicious the meat will taste.

The person before you showed that he or she is proud of successful experiments producing electrical sparks, pantomimed boasting to friends that he or she would use electricity to kill a turkey, and showed them how tender and delicious the meat would taste.

You come to the center of the room and pantomime attaching wires to the turkey, not paying attention because you are busy answering friends' questions, and falling to the ground from an electrical shock.

The person before you pantomimed attaching wires to a turkey, not paying attention because he or she was busy answering friends' questions, and falling to the ground from an electrical shock.

You come to the center of the room and pantomime writing, with a quill pen, a list of similarities between electricity and lightning and then making drawings of an experiment.

The person before you pantomimed writing, with a quill pen, a list of similarities between electricity and lightning and then making drawings of an experiment.

You come to the center of the room and pantomime making a kite.

The person before you pantomimed making a kite.

You come to the center of the room and pantomime adding a cotton string, a silk thread, and a metal key to a kite.

The person before you pantomimed adding a cotton string, a silk thread, and a metal key to a kite.

You come to the center of the room and pantomime standing under a barn roof and watching the rain and lightning during a storm.

The person before you pantomimed standing under a barn roof and watching the rain and lightning during a storm.

You come to the center of the room and pantomime flying the kite and holding tightly onto the silk thread.

The person before you pantomimed flying a kite and holding tightly onto a silk thread.

You come to the center of the room and pantomime moving your hand toward the metal key and then jerking your hand away quickly as sparks jump from the key to your fingers.

The person before you pantomimed moving his or her hand toward the metal key and then jerking the hand away quickly as sparks jumped from the key to his or her fingers.

You come to the center of the room and pantomime inventing the lightning rod.

The person before you pantomimed inventing the lightning rod.

You come to the center of the room and pantomime giving a speech about electricity to other scientists.

Elements of Weather

(Name Game)

Each child is given a 4" × 6" card for this activity. Ask the children to draw something depicting a weather event, such as a big snowflake, raindrop, hail, cloud, sunshine, tornado, cyclone, or hurricane. Place names on the front side of the pictures, leaving room for the rhythmic notation of their names. See the following illustration.

Advancing Skills:

★ To study the similarities and differences in weather conditions, the following activity may spark discovery discussions:

Read the following cards which give clues and ask children to move on each applicable clue and get to know their weather-mates:

1. I am wet. Meet me at the back of the room.
2. I am hot. Meet me at the front of the room.
3. I am noisy. Meet me by the door.
4. I am windy. Meet me by the windows.
5. I am windy and wet. Meet me in the center of the room.

Ask the children in each of those groups what is the best way to stay safe in those weather conditions.

★ Listen to "Cloudburst" from Grofe's ***Grand Canyon Suite***. Challenge the children to listen for and identify the rhythms of their names in the music. Plan a creative movement to depict the stages of the storm. Invite children who have traveled to describe desert weather.

Rainstorm

(Body Sounds)

This activity extends the knowledge of children and involves making a sound storm from body sounds. First, discuss the various stages which storms may have. Ask the children to plan with you a three–part storm that will be performed through body sounds alone. Explore all possible sounds that can be made with the body to depict wind, soft raindrops, large and heavy rain splats, thunder, *etc*.

1. Plan the first part of the storm with the wind kicking up, small intermittent raindrops, distant thunder, and medium drops falling steadily.

2. The second stage of the storm has stronger wind, heavy continuous rainfall, and loud thunder.

3. The third part is a gradual tapering of wind and rain. The thunder discontinues. The storm closes gently.

Discuss with the children the elements of sounds which they can control in their body sounds: the selected sound (tone color), the volume (dynamics), the speed of sound (tempo), and the number of sounds at once (texture).

Advancing Skills:

★ Try a rainstorm that has a different ordering of events. Contrast performances of sudden violent storms and abruptly ending storms. Tape-record their created storms to compare and re-check observations. Discuss different types of clouds that would signal foul weather.

★ As described in the previous activity, plan a rainstorm for performance using found sounds in the classroom. Find different ways of making "wind" sounds, explore a variety of raindrop noises, and select numerous thunder sounds of differing intensities. Organize the sounds into a multiple-stage storm.

★ Tape-record the performance and discuss the sound effects. Critique what effects were successful and what could be improved.

★ Listen to "Storm" from *The Little Mermaid* and choreograph a brief dance to depict the activity of the storm.

Swimming Pool

(Finger Play)

Associating summer and swimming in an outdoor pool is one way children can join a favorite activity to the appropriate season.

Swimming pool,	(Make swimming motion.)
Swimming pool,	(Make swimming motion.)
Clear blue water	(Place hand above eyes to shade them.)
Keeps us cool.	(Fan self with hand.)
Floating toys,	(Swat back and forth with arms outstretched.)
A bright beach ball,	(Form "O" shape with hands.)
Summer's the best	(Dance in place.)
Time of all.	

Invite the children to create a finger play for the other three seasons, for example, shoveling snow, raking leaves, planting seeds. Ask the children to sequence the finger plays in the order in which the seasons occur.

The Snow Is Dancing

(Creative Movement)

Depending upon the weather, our outdoor movements change. Imagine walking through a field of crispy leaves, heavy snow, dry hot sand, or a deep puddle of muddy rain. Each walk would differ markedly. Debussy wrote a delightful composition entitled *The Snow Is Dancing*, which will stimulate new ways to think about dancing in the cold outdoors.

Listen to the brief composition and notice the tempo for clues as to how fast to dance. Ask the children to demonstrate how heavy the snow is. What evidence can they find in the music? How can they show that feeling in their movements? Which way is the snow dancing?

The children may wish to make snowflakes to move during the performance. In an art lesson, fold squares (approximately twelve inches) of lightweight paper three times so that the paper has eight sections. Cut out designs on the edges of the wedge. See illustration below.

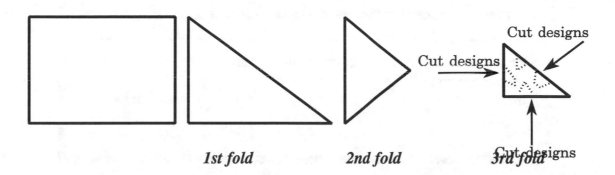

1st fold   *2nd fold*   *3rd fold*

Season Sights

(Pantomime)

This pantomime activity appeals to both beginning and advanced readers. For those just learning, the actions can be graphically represented and the pantomime sentence written beneath the picture on a student's card. For older children, the picture can be omitted and only the sentence retained. The activity combines reading, dramatic action, and science as children engage in these "seasonal" activities.

To play, place each picture and sentence or sentence only on an index card and distribute the cards so that each player has one. Ask for volunteers to pantomime the actions on their cards. The children watching should orally identify the action and the season in which it is most likely to occur.

Come to the center of the room and pantomime building a snowman.

Come to the center of the room and pantomime sledding down a hill.

Come to the center of the room and pantomime shoveling the sidewalk.

Come to the center of the room and pantomime scoring a goal in ice hockey.

Come to the center of the room and pantomime planting flowers in a garden.

Come to the center of the room and pantomime riding a bicycle.

Come to the center of the room and pantomime flying a kite.

Come to the center of the room and pantomime walking in a rain shower and playing in the puddles.

Come to the center of the room and pantomime raking leaves and hopping on a big pile of them.

Advancing Skill:

★ Make new cards using suggestions from the children and play the activity again using the new sentences. Prompt those watching to identify both the action and the season for each of the new sentences.

Time, Place, Action

(Pantomime)

This activity clarifies changes in the sun's position. You will need a flashlight and a set of pantomime cards for this activity. First, review directions in the classroom (north, south, east, and west). Discuss where the sun rises, sets, and various other locations throughout the day and night.

Assign children to work in cooperative groups of three or four. One child should be designated the light person. He or she controls the flashlight which provides an important clue in the pantomime. That child flashes the light to indicate possible sun position. Each team will be given a pantomime card, such as one in the examples below, and plays the scene. The light person shines the flashlight for the time clue. The other children act out the pantomime. After each group rehearses the pantomime, they perform it for the other groups to observe. Possible pantomime cards are:

> You are brushing your teeth at 7:00 A.M. (Action: Flashlight shines in the east. Children squeeze toothpaste from tube and brush teeth while looking at the mirror. Since children brush their teeth at all different times, the observant children should determine not only the pantomime action but also the approximate time.)

> You are reading the newspaper at 8:00 P.M.

> You are taking your little brother for a walk in the buggy at noon.

> You and your dog go for a run at 10:00 A.M.

> You are washing dinner dishes at 7:00 P.M.

> You are dreaming about a new mountain bike at 12:00 A.M.

> You are scrubbing the kitchen floor at 3:00 P.M.

Maui Nooses the Sun

(pronounced Ma-u-i) (Pantomime)

This Maori legend from New Zealand explains how the length of a day came to be. We suggest playing this first in unison, with each of the children playing Maui. Later, the legend can be replayed with individual casting of one child per role. Sidecoaching comments and questions often result in richer characterizations and suggested sidecoaching appears here in parenthesis.

You are Maui and you can do great deeds. You can change yourself from a man to a bird and back into a man again. (What do you look like when you are a bird?) You know many tricks. (What kind of magic can you do?) You think that nothing can conquer you. (Show how brave and smart you are.)

Today, you are sad. You watch the sun. (The glare is very bright.) It speeds across the sky so quickly that the people in your village cannot plant their crops. The sun burns so brightly that all of the water sources in your village have become dry. (How can you show that you are hot and thirsty?) Soon, you fear, there will be nothing to eat or drink and you are angry. You decide to teach the sun a lesson.

You think of a plan. You go to your brothers and ask them to help you. Although they respect your powers, they laugh at you. (How does this make you feel?) "Maui," your brothers say, "the sun is also strong and powerful. You cannot tame the sun." You proudly show them the magic jawbone you possess. (How can you show that you are proud of the jawbone?) "I can slow the sun's journey across the sky," you tell them, "but you must help me."

Your brothers agree to help. (How does this make you feel?) You ask them to braid ropes and show them how to make many different kinds. You all work busily. (What do you do while your brothers work?) At the end of the day, there are many coils of strong rope. You are tired and go to sleep.

The next morning, you and your brothers pick up the ropes and journey east, looking for the sun. (Some of you are walking quickly; others move more slowly. How do the ropes feel in your hands?) At the end of the day, you arrive at the edge of a pit surrounded by barren land. You point to it. "The sun rises from here," you tell your brothers.

You and your brothers work hard. You place posts around the pit and string the ropes around the posts until the area looks like a large cobweb. You make a noose from the strongest rope. At the first light, you caution your brothers to be quiet. (How can you do this without letting the sun know you are there?)

Soon, the sun begins to rise up from the pit. The rays are so bright that you and your brothers must shield your eyes. (How do the sun's rays make you feel?) You quickly adjust your vision. As soon as the sun's shoulders emerge and his head appears in the noose, you yell, "Pull!" and your brothers tighten the bonds.

The sun struggles. He threatens you. (How do you feel?) You use your magic jawbone to scare the sun until he agrees to do as you ask.

You tell the sun to move more slowly across the sky. You tell the sun to give people time to plant the fields and harvest the crops. The sun agrees to be a friend to mankind. (How can you show the sun that this promise pleases you?)

You release the sun from the ropes and he takes his place in the sky. You and your brothers return triumphantly to your village.

Interviewing Inventors

(Characterization)

Combine learning to use the library and making oral book reports with learning about inventions that have changed our lives. Before playing this activity, children should select one of the following inventors and read about that person and his or her invention.

> Marie Curie — chemical processes, geiger counter
> Alexander Graham Bell — the telephone
> Alice Chatham — the astronaut's helmet
> Henry Ford — the automobile
> The Wright Brothers — the airplane
> Thomas Alva Edison — the electric light bulb
> Jonas Salk — the polio vaccine
> Rose O'Neill — the Kewpie doll
> Rear Admiral Grace Murray Hopper — the computer program compiler

Once the children know the inventor and the invention well enough to discuss them with classmates, pair the students. One child assumes the role of the inventor and the other child assumes the role of the interviewer. Together, they develop and rehearse questions and responses for a radio or television talk show. These are then performed for the class. If the children are interested in switching roles, replay the activity, giving both students an opportunity to become the inventor that he or she has studied.

During the next phase, the children imagine that they are inventors. They are to develop a fictitious individual. They then create an autobiography for the inventor they imagine themselves to be and think of an invention for which they are famous. What have they invented? What does it do? After the children have had adequate time to develop the character and to become familiar with the invention, use the interview format as previously described.

Advancing Skill:

★ Combine the two exercises by performing a television news show in which Bell, Ford, and other real inventors are interviewed. Between the interview segments, have the children perform commercials for the new devices that their imaginary inventors have developed.

Rain, Snow

(Quieting Activities)

Children will be quiet and still after completing each of these weather related rests.

You are a snowflake falling from the sky and melting when you touch the ground.

You are a snowball melting into a puddle.

You are drops of rain gently falling onto the ground and spreading into a puddle.

You are a drop of rain freezing into a patch of ice.

Chapter 8

SOCIAL STUDIES

Content	Music/Creative Drama	
Forms of Transportation	Name Game:	Transportation Vehicles
	Song:	Down by the Station
	Pantomime:	Wheels
Careers and Employability	Finger Play:	Lots of Busy Folks
	Pantomime:	When I Grow Up
		Nonsense Occupations
	Living Pictures:	The Store
Multicultural Awareness: Israeli, American, Australian, Spanish, Native American, Japanese, Russian, German, African	Songs:	Mama Paquita
		Oh, Susanna
		Kookaburra
		Cascabel
		Michael, Row the Boat Ashore
		Pipe Dance Song
		Sakura
		Some Love Coffee
		The Farmyard
		Mos' Mos'
		Deaf Woman's Courtship
		Zum Gali Gali
		The Birch Tree
		Rocky Mountain
		Clementine
		Ach Ja
Citizenship	Sequence Game:	Pledge of Allegiance
	Story Creation and Dramatization:	Home is America Now
Judicial System	Characterization:	On Trial
U.S. Geography	Living Pictures:	Topography
		What State Am I?
	Musical Puzzles:	Chain Game

continued

Content	Music/Creative Drama	
World Geography	Concentration Game:	I've Been on a Trip to . . .
Relationships	Song: Improvisation:	Around the World in Eighty Ways What Will You Do?
Communication Networks	Characterization:	Radio Station T-R-I-P
Reference Materials	Characterization:	What's Our Line?

eachers will feel at home using music and creative drama in social studies lessons. In many ways, the performing arts are vehicles that lead to social experiences through song, dance, and story dramatization. Other units of instruction, including forms of transportation, citizenship, geography, and the judicial system, can be enhanced through activities that make remote or abstract concepts more understandable and enjoyable.

Transportation Vehicles

(Name Game)

This name tag activity is fun for the first day of school. Ask the children to imagine how they might travel to school. Draw the form of transportation large enough to be placed on a card along with their names. (Index cards are suggested.)

Typically, some children draw vehicles from the present or past such as race cars or chariots. Some children draw animals and others draw vehicles for the future. Give each child a chance to introduce him- or herself and the form of transportation chosen. Children also may make a time line from the various cards, placing covered wagons and trains of the past before rockets of the future.

Advancing Skills:

★ After listening to "On the Trail" from Grofe's **Grand Canyon Suite**, invite the children to draw pictures of the Grand Canyon from the perspective of their chosen vehicle such as a boat in the river at the bottom of the canyon or a helicopter midway up the canyon walls.

★ Provide an opportunity for children to locate pictures of Marshall M. Frederick's sculptures related to the history of transportation. Ask them to imagine traveling, using one of the modes represented, and to describe to classmates what the travel experience entails.

★ Bring to the children's attention the correlation between the development of modes of transportation and the use/mastery of raw materials and technology. Hot air balloons, for example, were not used until what processes were refined?

Down by the Station

(Song)

This is a simple round for little voices, however, the children are bound to want to dramatize the events.

Advancing Skills:

★ Ask the children to move only their feet to the rhythm and simulate train wheels moving to the jerky rhythm:

★ Ask the children to describe different types of trains (electric, toy, underground, steam-powered, *etc*.). What features are essentially the same?

Wheels
(Pantomime)

The wheel is one of humankind's greatest inventions, and children recognize its importance to migration, settlement, and culture when their social studies units include content on transportation by wheeled vehicles. The pioneers present a vivid picture, for example, moving westward in their conestoga wagons, wheels turning.

The following pantomime may be used as a warm-up activity for studying forms of transportation, as the wheels here are attached to modes of transportation familiar to the children or easily researched. They should pantomime the movement or image associated with each form of transportation as the piece is narrated. The children may wish to say in unison, "The wheels go 'round and 'round," after each action. Although speaking is not in keeping with pantomime, in this case it is an appropriate accompaniment to the activity.

Aaron steers an ambulance,
The wheels go 'round and 'round.

Bonnie bounces on a bicycle,
The wheels go 'round and 'round.

Calvin cavorts in a carriage,
The wheels go 'round and 'round.

Darnell drives a dump truck,
The wheels go 'round and 'round.

Elaine travels on an elevated train,
The wheels go 'round and 'round.

Frank rotates on a ferris wheel,
The wheels go 'round and 'round.

George goes by on a go-cart,
The wheels go 'round and 'round.

Harvey hires a hansom,
The wheels go 'round and 'round.

Inez chugs along in an ironhorse,
The wheels go 'round and 'round.

Justin journeys in a jeep,
The wheels go 'round and 'round.

Kellie bikes with kickstand up,
The wheels go 'round and 'round.

Louie lingers in a limo,
The wheels go 'round and 'round.

Michael maneuvers a motorcycle,
The wheels go 'round and 'round.

Norma's car has non-skid tires,
The wheels go 'round and 'round.

Oprah waves from an open car,
The wheels go 'round and 'round.

Paul sails on a paddlewheeler,
The wheels go 'round and 'round.

Queenie's race car's fast as quicksilver,
The wheels go 'round and 'round.

Robert rides a rickshaw,
The wheels go 'round and 'round.

Shirley commutes on a school bus,
The wheels go 'round and 'round.

Tanya travels in a taxi,
The wheels go 'round and 'round.

Ursula balances upon a unicycle,
The wheels go 'round and 'round.

Vanessa ventures in a van,
The wheels go 'round and 'round.

Willie wanders in a wheelchair,
The wheels go 'round and 'round.

X, Y, and Z are mysteries,
What wheels go 'round and 'round?

Advancing Skill:

★ Play this activity as a name game. With the children seated in a circle, ask each to say his or her first name, an appropriate verb, and an object with wheels that begins with the same letter as the child's name.

Example:

My name is Walter. I ride in a wagon.

Lots of Busy Folks

(Finger Play)

It is fun for children to imagine what career they might have when they are older. This finger play presents some options.

Lots of busy folks at work,	(Count the fingers on one hand.)
Lots of jobs to do.	(Count the fingers on the other hand.)
Working can be lots of fun.	(Smile.)
Which job is for you?	(Shrug shoulders.)
Waitresses bring people food.	(Serve imaginary plate.)
Tellers count the change.	(Hand imaginary coin to the person next to you.)
Travel agents help with trips.	
Flights they can arrange.	(Spread arms and fly in place.)
Cars and trucks mechanics fix.	(Make steering motion with hands.)
Movie stars have fame.	(Strike a glamorous pose.)
Reporters cover stories.	(Write on an imaginary note pad.)
Athletes play in games.	(Make "v" for "victory" sign with fingers.)
Lots of busy folks at work,	(Count the fingers on one hand.)
Lots of jobs to do.	(Count the fingers on the other hand.)
Are there other jobs you'd like?	(Point to person next to you.)
Which job is for you?	(Shrug shoulders.)

Advancing Skill:

★ Lead a discussion in which the children volunteer things they like to do. What kind of job would involve those skills or activities? Invite a demonstration of these occupations using pantomimed actions.

When I Grow Up

(Pantomime)

Place each of the verses of the poem on an index card and have each student take one. The child pantomimes the verse on his or her card.

When I grow up
I want to be
A famous person
On TV.

When I grow up
I want to be
A sailor on
The rolling sea.

When I grow up
I want to be
A locksmith fixing
Doors and keys.

When I grow up
I want to be
A forester
Protecting trees.

When I grow up
I want to be
Making music
In all keys.

When I grow up
I want to be
A tailor
Of dungarees.

When I grow up
I want to be
A beekeeper
With honey.

When I grow up
I want to be
A writer
Telling fantasies.

When I grow up
I want to be
A zookeeper
With chimpanzees.

When I grow up
I want to be
A surgeon
Mending knees.

When I grow up
I want to be
An astronaut
Feeling "g"s.

When I grow up
I want to be
Elected by
Majority.

When I grow up
I want to be
A teacher of
Technology.

When I grow up
I want to be
A valuable
Employee.

When I grow old
I want to see
That I pleased others
As well as me.

Advancing Skill:

★ As a class, construct a new poem using other occupations. Use the same format of one verse per index card. Play the new poem in unison. Then distribute the cards so that, as a replay, each child can individually pantomime a verse.

Nonsense Occupations

(Pantomime)

Provide two stacks of cards for the children. One stack should be animal cards, with the name and/or picture of an animal on each. The other stack should have cards identifying occupations and/or showing pictures of people doing particular jobs. A child should draw a card from each stack and then, in pantomime, show the animal character engaged in the occupation. The other children can guess what animal the child is portraying and what job he or she is doing.

Animals	Occupations
monkey	teacher
bird	construction worker
fish	secretary
giraffe	farmer

Advancing Skill:

★ If the children enjoy infusing animal characters with human qualities, they can create *The Crazy Mall*. Boys and girls can become clerks, customers, food vendors, *etc.*, and each character must be an animal with human qualities. The children next can improvise stories about what might happen at this kind of a mall when these characters interact with one another.

The Store
(Living Pictures)

How many different kinds of stores can children name? Do they know who works and shops in each? Have the children create living pictures of stores. They might, for example, create one of a grocery store or a clothing store. Included in the living picture should be employees and customers, as well as objects which identify the place.

Mama Paquita
(Song)

Children will grasp this song quickly due to its catchy lyrics. Its content gives clues as to its cultural origin.

Additional Verses:

2. Mama Paquita, Mama Paquita,
    Mama Paquita, buy your baby some pajamas,
    Some new pajamas, and a sombrero,
    A new sombrero that your baby will enjoy,
        ma-ma-ma-ma.

Mama Paquita, Mama Paquita,
Mama Paquita says, "I haven't any money
To buy pajamas and a sombrero,
Let's go to Carnival and dance the
    night away!"

Advancing Skills:

★ The children clap three times after the close of each phrase (marked with X's above.)

★ Discuss terms that are cultural in the song. Find out where Brazil is, why a sombrero is desirable, and where papayas grow.

★ What type of instruments might be used in South America to accompany this song? Research and make tambourines, castanets, drums, and other instruments that fit the cultural integrity.

Oh, Susanna
(Song)

Notice that this song by a famous American composer, Stephen Foster, has two sections: part A contains the verses; part B contains the chorus. This is a common form to songs, allowing stories to be told with a recurring refrain. Bring this to the children's attention as you introduce the song to them.

Additional Verses:

2. I had a dream the other night
    When ev'rything was still;
    I thought I saw Susanna
    A comin' down the hill;
    The buckwheat cake was in her mouth,
    The tear was in her eye;
    Says I, I'm comin' from the south,
    Susanna, don't you cry.
    O, Susanna, O don't you cry for me,
    I've come from Alabama
    With my banjo on my knee.

3. I soon will be in New Orleans,
    And then I'll look around,
    And when I find Susanna
    I'll fall upon the ground.
    And if I do not find her,
    This darky'll surely die,
    And when I'm dead and buried,
    Susanna, don't you cry.
    O, Susanna, O don't you cry for me,
    I've come from Alabama
    With my banjo on my knee.

Advancing Skills:

★ Add body sounds to the chorus on the beat. Try alternating one-hand patschen and clapping with a one-foot stamping on the patschen. This configuration was used many years ago with folk songs.

★ Ask the children to each create their own body sound for the verse.

★ On a map, trace a possible route from Alabama to New Orleans. What form of transportation would someone take on this route in 1800? 1900? 2000?

> The set of songs which follow are rich in unfolding interesting information about different cultures. Once the songs are taught, children invariably ask about the vocabulary or meaning. With a sense of curiosity and excited discovery, explore children's questions, or devise questions to lead the children's curiosity. Appreciation of cultural differences is the goal. Independent research may be prompted. Deeper understanding will result.

Kookaburra

(Song)

This Australian folk tune[1] is a round. Children will be successful singing it if they know the melody line very well. Give them many opportunities to sing it alone before dividing the group and performing it as a round.

Khu- kha- ba- ra lik- ka- lan- ga o - mu- sa - la, Bu- san- ga- li om- wa- mi e - shi - a - lo.

Tse - ka, khu- kha- ba - ra, Tse - ka, khu- kha- ba- ra, Mi rem - be men - u - bwo.

Translation:

> Kookaburra sits in an old gum tree,
> Merry, merry king of the bush!
> Laugh, kookaburra, laugh, kookaburra!
> Gay your life must be!

---

[1] uses the Swahili dialect of the Luhya people

Advancing Skills:

⭐ Perform the round by clapping it, then sing and clap, finally sing without clapping.

⭐ Research what a gum tree is.

⭐ Research Australian animals. Ask the children to study the following animals and then to move as each animal and to show, in pantomime, something that the animal might do. A koala, for example, might sit in a gum tree savoring a gum leaf in its mouth.

Animals: koala, kookaburra, wombat, Tasmanian devil, kangaroo, magpie, sulphur crested cockatoo, emu

Cascabel
(Song) (to the tune of *Jingle Bells*)

Learn some Spanish words for this familiar tune:

Cascabel, cascabel, musica de amor,
Dulces horas, gratas, horas, juventud en flor,
Cascabel, cascabel, tan sentimental,
No dejes casbelita de repiquetar.

Advancing Skills:

⭐ Play jingle bells or jingle clogs in the following ostinato (repeated) pattern:

⭐ Invite family members of students who speak other foreign languages to provide words for this tune or other familiar songs. If appropriate, teach the children the new song.

Michael, Row the Boat Ashore

(Song)

This song is a stimulus for musical improvisation. Assign the children to work in pairs after knowing the song well. Have them get acquainted with one another by exchanging their favorite hobby, sport, or artistic activity. Invite the children to sit in a circle and sing the information they learned about their partner, creating new lyrics for the tune which follows. For example: "Frances plays piano well, Hallelujah." Or "Sun-Jae likes karate class, Hallelujah."

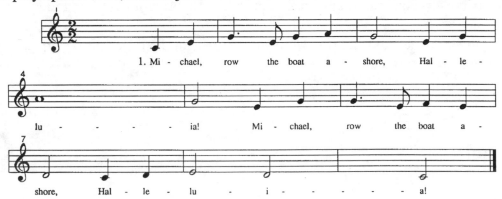

Additional Verses:

2. Jordan River is deep and wide,
   Halleluia!
   Jordan River is deep and wide,
   Halleluia!

3. Gabriel, blow the trumpet horn,
   Halleluia!
   Gabriel, blow the trumpet horn,
   Halleluia!

4. Trumpet sounds the world around,
   Halleluia!
   Trumpet sounds the world around,
   Halleluia!

5. Michael, haul the boat ashore,
   Halleluia!
   Michael, haul the boat ashore,
   Halleluia!

Pipe Dance Song

(Song)

The following Native American tune lends itself to an accompaniment with a steady drum beat. Notice the traditional pattern, accenting the first beat of the four-beat pattern. After the song is learned, invite students to choreograph a dance.

Advancing Skills:

★ After the teacher models a new ostinato for drums to accompany the song, invite the children to invent one of their own.

★ After translating the language, sing the song with English lyrics composed by the students.

Sakura

(Song)

This song uses the uppermost pitches of children's vocal ranges. It is a characteristic Japanese folk song with simple rhythms moving smoothly. Traditionally, the song is performed slowly.

Advancing Skills:

★ Notice the markings for dynamics. Perform the song as indicated (f=loud, p=soft, m=medium, and dim.=gradually softer).

★ Where are cherry trees grown in the United States? Locate these sites on a map.

★ Find examples of the cherry blossom used in Japanese art. What type of climate is required for cherry trees to grow in Japan?

Some Love Coffee

(Song)

This little song is over 100 years old. It looks simple, however, it changes meter as the lyrics change.

Because the meter signature indicates a half note (♩) equals one beat, the quarter note (♪) gets one half of the beat. The syllables for performing the rhythm are then:

$$♩ = \text{ta}$$

$$♪♪ = \text{ti ti}$$

$$♫♫ = \text{ti ri ti ri}$$

Use the rhythmic syllables to read the song.

You may feel as though the song isn't finished at the end. This is because it ends on a tone other than the pitch in which the song is keyed. Try singing the first line again after the second to achieve an ABA form.

Advancing Skill:

★ Many pioneers (women and men) often sang when they were lonely. Why might they be lonely? What are some activities in which pioneers engage?

The Farmyard
(Song)

Gr. K-3

Children have been singing this song for over 100 years, too. Its appeal lies in the infinite number of sounds they can supply for the animals.

1. Had me a cat and the cat pleased me, Fed my cat in yon - ders tree; The cat went fid - dle - i - dee.

2. Had me a dog and the dog pleased me, Fed my dog in yon - ders tree; The dog went boo, boo, boo, And the cat went fid - dle - i - dee. hog went kru - si, kru - si, kru - si, The

Additional Verses:

3. The hen went ka, ka, ka.
4. The hog went kru-si, kru-si, kru-si.
5. The sheep went baa, baa, baa.

6. The cow went moo, moo, moo.
7. The calf went ma, ma, ma.

Advancing Skill:

★ Animals have always been an important part of our cultural history. Some animals were part of livestock raised for slaughter. Other animals were "working" members (work horses, prairie dogs, hunting dogs, *etc.*). Yet other animals were pets. Invite the children to research one type of animal for its various roles throughout history.

Mos' Mos'

(Song)

"Mos'" means cat; "nya" means meow! This Native American song tells about a cat who steals a sheepskin.

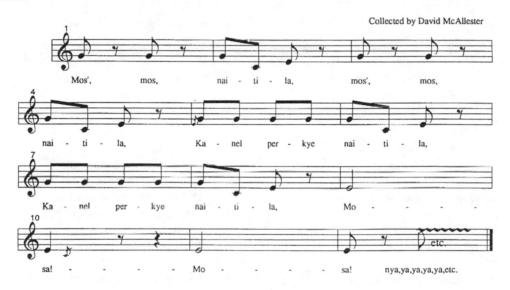

Collected by David McAllester

Mos', mos, nai - ti - la, mos', mos,

nai - ti - la, Ka - nel per - kye nai - ti - la,

Ka - nel per - kye nai - ti - la, Mo - - -

sa! - - - Mo - - - sa! nya, ya, ya, ya, ya, etc.

Translation:

Mos', mos', naitila, mos', mos', naitila,	(Cat, cat, steals, cat, cat steals,)
Kanelperkye naitila, kanelperkye naitila,	(Sheepskin, steals, Sheepskin, steals,)
Mo-sa! Mo-sa! Nya, nya, nya, nya, nya, . . .	(Ca—t! Ca—t! Meow, meow, meow . . .)

Deaf Woman's Courtship

(Song)

This conversation song tells the age-old story of men's and women's courting interests. It also provides a little history of women's work with wool.

1. Old wom-an, old wom-an, Are you fond of card - ing?
Old wom-an, old wom-an, Are you fond of card - ing?
Speak a lit - tle loud - er, sir! I'm ver - y hard of hear - ing.

Additional Verses:

2. Old woman, old woman,
    Are you fond of spinning?
    Old woman, old woman,
    Are you fond of spinning?
    Speak a little louder, sir!
    I'm very hard of hearing.

3. Old woman, old woman,
    Will you darn my stocking?
    Old woman, old woman,
    Will you darn my stocking?
    Speak a little louder, sir!
    I'm very hard of hearing.

4. Old woman, old woman,
    Will you let me court you?
    Old woman, old woman,
    Will you let me court you?
    Speak a little louder, sir!
    I just begin to hear you.

5. Old woman, old woman,
    Don't you want to marry me?
    Old woman, old woman,
    Don't you want to marry me?
    Oh, my goodness gracious me!
    I think that now I hear you!

Break the class into a boys' chorus and girls' chorus. Have the boys sing the questions and the girls sing the responses. Each verse is progressively louder until the final one. Boys sing the final verse softly; girls respond loudly.

Advancing Skills:

★ Discuss the process of wool working in each verse.

★ The children might create words for an "Old Farmer Courtship" version—with four verses of farming duties before the final proposal question.

★ Invite the children to pantomime the action of the song.

Zum Gali Gali
(Song)

Children make *Zum Gali Gali* one of their favorites as soon as they learn it. The Israeli folk song should be sung rather quickly, however, take care that the speed doesn't run away! A hand jive to keep the beat may assist.

Israeli Round

Zum ga - li ga - li ga - li, Zum ga - li ga - li. Zum ga - li ga - li ga - li,

Zum ga - li ga - li. 1. He cha - lutz le 'man a - vo - dah:

A - vo - dah le 'man he - cha - lutz.

Additional Verses:

2. Avodah le 'man hechalutz:
   Hechalutz le 'man avodah.

3. Hechalutz le 'man habtulah:
   Habtulah le 'man hechalutz.

4. Hashalom le 'man ha'amim:
   Ha'amim le 'man hashalom.

The Birch Tree
(Song)

This Russian folk song's topic is one of that country's greatest natural resources: birch trees.

Russian Folk Song

Sil - ver birch a - lone in the mead - ow.

Stand - ing all a - lone in the mead - ow.

Lone - - - ly birch tree in the mead - ow.

Love - - - ly birch tree in the mead - ow.

Advancing Skills:

★ Ask the children to research indigenous trees for continents they study, *e.g.*, gum trees, rubber trees, rain forest trees, *etc*.

★ Challenge the children to sing the song using rhythmic syllables.

★ Invite the children to research local and regional natural resources. Make up a new verse using these resources with lyrics to fit *The Birch Tree* melody. Teach the class the "local" verses with the integrated research.

Rocky Mountain

(Song)

Rocky Mountain has plenty of appeal to youngsters. Note the AB form (verse and refrain) when teaching this American tune to the children.

Additional Verse:

2.   Rocky mountain, rocky mountain, rocky mountain sky,
     When you reach that rocky mountain spread your wings and fly.

Advancing Skills:

★ On the refrain (B), fill in rests with sounds from wooden rhythm instruments.

★ Sing the first note of each measure in the refrain with a slight accent to stress the beat. Stamp your feet on the beat as well.

★ Listen to the melodic contour of the song as you sing it in slow motion. Place the following arches on the chalkboard and ask the children to identify the lines of the song that belong to the following contours:

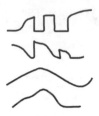

★ Ask the children to research the Rocky Mountains, determining location, heights, *etc*. Which of the previous melodic contours seems to suggest the shape of these mountains?

Clementine

(Song)

Sing *Clementine* feeling the triple meter.

1. In a cav - ern by a can - yon, Ex - ca - vat - ing for a mine, Dwelt a min - er, for - ty - nin - er, And his daugh - ter, Clem - en - tine.

Refrain:

Oh, my darling, oh, my darling,
Oh, my darling Clementine,
You are lost and gone forever,
Dreadful sorry, Clementine.

2. Light she was and like a feather,
   And her shoes were number nine;
   Herring boxes without topses,
   Sandals were for Clementine.

3. Drove she ducklings to the water
   Every morning just at nine;
   Struck her foot against a splinter,
   Fell into the foaming brine.

4. Rosy lips above the water
   Blowing bubbles mighty fine;
   But, alas! I was no swimmer,
   So I lost my Clementine.

Advancing Skills:

 Accompany the song with a hand jive that is made up of three movements. One example might be: patschen, slap, snap. One hundred and fifty years ago, miners sang this tune. How might they have accompanied it?

 The teacher conducts the song. Use the following gesture:

Note that the song begins with an incomplete measure. The first full measure for the conducting beat starts on "cavern."

 Research mining activities in various parts of the world. Discuss different elements (diamonds, coal, aluminum, *etc.*) that are mined.

Ach Ja
(Song)

Fairs have been part of many children's lives for over a century. This song suggests children join in friendship at the fair.

1. When my fath-er and my moth-er are a-go-ing to the fair, Ach
ja! Ach ja! If they have-n't an-y mon-ey, they're as rich as an-y there, Ach
ja! Ach ja! Tra la la, Tra la la, Tra la la la la la la Tra la
la, Tra la la Tra la la la la la la, Ach ja! Ach ja!

Additional Verse:

2.   It is fun to join the people who are hurrying to the fair, Ach ja! Ach ja!
     And to know that friends and neighbors will be waiting for you there, Ach ja! Ach ja!

Form two lines with four children (four girls/four boys) in each line facing one another. Girls have hands on hips. Boys place one arm folded across front, the other folded across back.

Line 1: Shuffle feet in position. "Ach Ja" boys bow; "Ach Ja" girls curtsy.

Line 2: Shuffle feet in position. "Ach Ja" same as above.

Line 3: Link arms (right elbows) with facing partners and skip clockwise.

Line 4: Link other arms (left elbows) with partner and skip other direction.

"Ach Ja" same as above.

Advancing Skills:

★ Discuss fairs—state fairs, county fairs, 4-H fairs. What is their purpose? Invite children to share their experiences participating in or attending fairs.

★ Toward the end of the academic year, plan a classroom fair. Determine with the children what the classroom community's accomplishments have been for the year. Plan and construct a fair which highlights these accomplishments. Invite family members to attend.

Pledge of Allegiance

(Sequence Game)

We suggest using this activity in conjunction with lessons on the history of the Pledge of Allegiance. In preparation for playing, children need to consult the encyclopedia and other reference sources for information on Francis Bellamy, President Benjamin Harrison, the origin of the Columbus Day holiday, *The Youth's Companion* magazine, and America in 1892. Findings can be presented in brief oral reports. Discuss any of the events on the sequence cards which may be unfamiliar to the children before commencing play.

You start the game. Come to the center of the room and pantomime a child opening his or her copy of *A Youth's Companion* and reading it.

The person before you pantomimed a child opening his or her copy of *A Youth's Companion* and reading it.

You come to the center of the room and pantomime a child going door to door and collecting pennies from neighbors.

The person before you pantomimed a child going door to door and collecting pennies from neighbors.

You come to the center of the room and pantomime counting your pennies, buying a flag, and then raising the flag in front of your school.

The person before you pantomimed counting pennies, buying a flag, and then raising the flag in front of the school.

You come to the center of the room and pantomime an earnest and determined Francis Bellamy convincing President Benjamin Harrison about an idea to celebrate a new holiday, Columbus Day, and then excitedly shaking the President's hand.

The person before you pantomimed an earnest and determined Francis Bellamy convincing President Benjamin Harrison about an idea to celebrate a new holiday, Columbus Day, and then excitedly shaking the President's hand.

You come to the center of the room and pantomime thirty-six-year-old Francis Bellamy sitting down at his desk on a warm August evening in 1892, writing the first pledge.

> *I pledge allegiance to my Flag*
> *and to the Republic*
> *for which it stands—*
> *one Nation indivisible—*
> *with liberty and justice for all.*

The person before you pantomimed thirty-six-year-old Francis Bellamy sitting down at his desk on a warm August evening in 1892, writing the first pledge.

> I pledge allegiance to my Flag
> and to the Republic
> for which it stands—
> one Nation indivisible—
> with liberty and justice for all.

You come to the center of the room and pantomime a teacher writing definitions to words in the pledge on the board and then calling on students to read the definitions.

The person before you pantomimed a teacher writing definitions to words in the pledge on the board and then calling on students to read the definitions.

You come to the center of the room, raise your right hand, keep your left hand at your side, and pantomime reciting the pledge as Francis Bellamy wrote it.

The person before you raised his or her right hand, kept the left hand at the side, and pantomimed reciting the pledge as Francis Bellamy wrote it.

You come to the center of the room and pantomime pounding a gavel at a meeting and then placing your right hand on your heart and reciting these beginning lines of the pledge.

> *I pledge allegiance to the flag*
> *of the United States of America.*

The person before you pantomimed pounding a gavel at a meeting and then placing his or her right hand on the heart and reciting these beginning lines of the pledge.

> I pledge allegiance to the flag
> of the United States of America.

You come to the center of the room and pantomime showing the number fifty with your fingers, blowing out candles on a birthday cake, and signing a paper which makes the pledge a part of national law.

The person before you pantomimed showing the number fifty with his or her fingers, blowing out candles on a birthday cake, and signing a paper which makes the pledge a part of national law.

You come to the center of the room and pantomime a Supreme Court Justice putting on a robe, taking a seat in the courtroom, and shaking your head from side to side to say, "No."

The person before you pantomimed a Supreme Court Justice putting on a robe, taking a seat in the courtroom, and shaking his or her head from side to side to say, "No."

You come to the center of the room and pantomime counting votes in Congress and then announcing that "one nation under God" has been added to the pledge.

The person before you pantomimed counting votes in Congress and then announcing that "one nation under God" has been added to the pledge.

You come to the center of the room and, aloud, lead classmates in reciting the Pledge of Allegiance.

> *I pledge allegiance to the flag*
> *of the United States of America*
> *and to the Republic*
> *for which it stands,*
> *one Nation under God,*
> *indivisible,*
> *with liberty and justice for all.*

Adapted from June Swanson, *I Pledge Allegiance*, Minneapolis: Carolrhoda Books, 1990.

Home is America Now
(Citizenship)

The children should work with this story in several ways in preparation for playing it as an original story to dramatize. Told from the protagonist's point of view, it encompasses some of the experiences of immigrants to the United States. Encourage the students to engage in empathic response when trying on the main character.

To begin, either the teacher or a student should read the story aloud to the class. Then, ask the children to search through magazines and newspapers for a picture of a child they think could be the speaker. After each student has located a picture, ask him or her to narrate the story again while showing the picture to the class. The student should use vocal characterization during this phase of the activity.

Next, invite the children to do library research about the country from which their selected person has immigrated. Use this as the basis of a television interview show, casting one student as the child and the other as the interviewer. Both students should respond as their respective characters. After playing once, switch roles so that both children have an opportunity to play an immigrating character.

Divide the children into small groups and ask each group to select one of the following scenes for story creation. Guide each group in determining the protagonist and additional characters needed for their story. What will be the conflict? What dialogue might the characters use? Give students time to develop and rehearse their story before playing it for the class.

> Scene #1: What is life like for your character before coming to the United States? Why are you leaving your native land?
>
> Scene #2: What is life in school like for you? What do you do during a typical school day?
>
> Scene #3: How do you maintain links to your former country? Do you go to a native school on weekends? What customs do you practice at home?
>
> Scene #4: How do you try to adjust to life in America? How do you practice for citizenship?

Finally, ask the children to use *Home Is America Now* as the basis for a story dramatization. They may wish to incorporate information, characters, and dialogue from previously played segments related to this culminating endeavor.

Home is America Now

Sometimes I remember how it was before we came here. My father would tell me, "My child, someday I will take you to America. There, we will have a better life."

We waited for several years before we could come. Now that we have finally arrived in America, my parents work two jobs each just so we will have enough money to live. It is hard for me at school because some of the other children laugh at me. I can't always understand them because I don't know English well. We don't speak English at home and that makes it more difficult for me to make friends.

One day, at school, some of the children used an expression that I didn't understand. They asked me if I was "cool." I didn't know what they meant and I answered, "No, I am warm, thank you." They laughed and laughed. It makes me feel sad and confused when they do this.

I have to study a lot. I have classes just like the other children at school, but I also get special tutoring because I need help understanding the language. Sometimes I am taken out of class by my tutor. We study by ourselves and she helps me with my English.

School isn't all bad, though. When we have "Show and Tell," I bring in things from my native country. All of my classmates are curious and I am eager to tell about my former home. I also like studying history and learning American customs. I know that, if I learn about this country, I will fit in more quickly.

I have to go to school on Saturday, too. My parents want me to know about my culture so I go to a special school where we learn about my former country. All of my classmates there are from my native land. We know many of the same games and customs that my new American friends don't know.

My parents study, too. When they have been here for five years, they will become naturalized citizens. They must, however, know the English language and American history and so they study, like me. They look forward to the day that they will raise their hands and take an oath that makes them citizens of the United States. I look forward to that, too, because, since I am their child, I will also become a citizen then. I know that we will be good Americans. This is our home now.

On Trial
(Characterization)

Experiencing the judicial system through a mock trial becomes a memorable event when the characters and the crime are taken from favorite verses. In the following activity, children should take a nursery rhyme, such as *Tom, Tom the Piper's Son* or *The Queen of Hearts*, in which a crime is described. They develop a court case around the scenario. In the former, for example, characters would include Tom, the attorneys, the judge, witnesses, and the jury. Class members build the story by determining certain circumstances. Why, for example, did Tom steal? Attorneys for each side have to build their case. The trial is then staged in the classroom.

Advancing Skill:

★ A variation to this activity could be played based upon classroom regulations or civics issues. In these variations, the issues may not be legal ones but would involve experiential learning related to rules.

Topography
(Living Pictures)

Children will be using their bodies to create pictures in this exercise designed to illustrate features of land and water areas such as a desert, the seashore, a lake, the mountains, a river, and so forth. Determine which topographical picture is to be created. Ask one child to begin by taking a position that suggests something or a part of something that would be in that scene. The child takes that position and freezes in place. As other children see how they might contribute to the picture, they join and freeze as in the following example.

One child stands straight with arms forming a triangle above his or her head, fingers touching. Two more children stand next to the first child, taking the same pose. Several other children lie in front of the three, forming a circle with their bodies. The picture is of a mountain with a lake in front of it.

What State Am I?
(Living Pictures)

What State Am I? is comparable to *Topography* in that both visually reinforce distinguishing features of land masses. In this activity, states serve as the stimulus for creating living pictures.

Students should work in small groups, with each group studying the outline of a particular state on a map. They then position themselves on the floor, recreating the state's contour with their bodies. Members of the other groups identify the state. Advanced players may wish to add topographical features such as mountains and rivers, also created by classmates' bodies.

Chain Game
(Musical Puzzles)

The chain game is a memory game. It involves recalling and repeating as many patterns as possible. As in concentration games, children will need to recall in proper order the responses of those who have preceded them.

Begin teaching the game with something simple such as the names of states. Ask children to work in groups of eight. The opening chant follows (each line is said by the leader and repeated by the group):

> Think of
> Names of
> Types of
> Kinds of
> STATES

Leader:	Mississippi			
Child 1:	Mississippi	Vermont		
Child 2:	Mississippi	Vermont	Idaho	
Child 3:	Mississippi	Vermont	Idaho	Arizona

The goal is for each child to continue the "chain" of information and add a new piece. The game continues until the beat is interrupted with a pause or memory lapse.

Any category of ideas to recall can be reviewed.

Advancing Skill:

★ Change the content to capitals, rivers, oceans, mountains, or other geographic information.

I've Been on a Trip to . . .

(Concentration Game)

This concentration game can help children to associate specific places with the products and resources found there. Ask the children to imagine that they are coming back from a trip or vacation. As the game is played, each repeats the opening and lists all of the items before adding a new one.

Example:

Teacher: I've been on a trip to Europe and I'm bringing home some crystal from Ireland.

Child 1: I've been on a trip to Europe and I'm bringing home some crystal from Ireland and a watch from Switzerland.

Child 2: I've been on a trip to Europe and I'm bringing home some crystal from Ireland, a watch from Switzerland, and a diamond from Amsterdam.

If a child forgets, encourage others to assist with clues or nonverbal descriptions of the items. If a child truly draws a blank, move on to the next person and continue the game or begin again.

After playing the concentration game, the students can test their research skills by selecting several of the items named which are created through manufacturing. Several research teams are formed and each team selects one of the items to investigate. Individual groups are responsible for learning about how their item is made and reporting the information to their classmates. In addition to oral content, teams should practice making a body sculpture of one of the machines used in the manufacturing process. Their report to the class should include a demonstration of their body sculpture machine, an explanation of how it works, and their report on the product.

Advancing Skill:

★ Use the game to reinforce learning about specific geographic regions. The exercise can be done by focusing upon a continent, region, country, state, or city. As a research project, children then investigate any of the products named to learn how they are manufactured or created. Findings are reported to the class. For this part of the exercise, students assume the character of an investigative reporter and deliver their story using the voice, speaking style, and physical stance of their journalistic sleuth.

Around the World in Eighty Ways

(Song)

It might be fun to begin this lesson listening to the song *Around the World in Eighty Days* from *The Roar of the Greasepaint . . . .* Because this song was written well before the concourse and lightning speed of satellites and spaceships, a discussion of how the speed of transportation has developed would be worthwhile. Soon, we may be able to travel around the world in eighty minutes!

The following activity will help students become aware of different continents and the ways in which the continents are connected to one another. This activity requires a globe for the teacher and blank world maps for each student. Children should be able to distinguish land and water masses on their maps. To travel across continents, one might cross rivers, mountains, lakes, and sometimes harbors, hopping to peninsulas, and so forth. To travel from one continent to another, one may travel by land or by sea. This activity raises the students' awareness of topical features on globes and maps by identifying how these features are depicted. Social studies skills are reinforced by filling in maps and singing songs or chants to clarify geographical features as the children "travel."

Start by selecting a continent. Travel from east to west as you examine the topographical features of that continent. Begin by singing the *Caisson Song* as you hike. Every time you must cross a river, sing the *Volga Boat Song*, *Sail Silver Moon Boat*, or *The Big Ship Sails*. Draw the river on the map. Notice how it curves and turns. Notice how the melody of the song goes up and down.

If you come across mountains, sing *Happy Wanderer*. Draw symbols to indicate mountains on the map. When singing the refrain of the song, notice how the song's contour is mountain-like, moving very high. *Going Over the Sea* can be sung if you need to travel over a sea to a new continent.

Depending upon the specific continent, select a song of that culture when placing major cities on the map. Many times the song will provide additional social studies content to integrate, such as customs, geography, and cultural insights. *Planting Rice Is Never Fun*, to illustrate, hints at the type of climate and terrain in the Philippines. A list of suggested songs and source books follows.

AFRICA
Counting Songs
Dipidu
Kum-Bah-Ya
Sing Noel
*Zambian Folk Song**

AUSTRALIA
Song of the Aboriginal Boy
Botany Bay
Waltzing Matilda

GREAT BRITAIN/IRELAND
Coventry Carol
Greensleeves
Scarborough Fair

CANADA
Crocodile Song
Jamboree

CARIBBEAN
Boysie
*Hurry**

CHINA
*Flower Drum Song**
*Love Song**
Sail Silver Moon Boat

EUROPE
*Are You Sleeping?** (French)
German Lullaby
Polish Hymn Tune
Peter and Pal (Hungarian)

INDIA
*Gup! Tall Tale**
*Indian Chant**

ISRAELI
*Hanukkah**
*Hava Nagila**
Toembai
*Zum Gali Gali**

JAPAN AND KOREA
*Cherry Bloom**
Japanese Rain Song
*Lullaby**

LATIN AMERICA AND MEXICO
  Chiapenecas*
  The Condor*
  Mexican Hat Dance
  The Tortillas Vendor*

MIDDLE EAST
  Beautiful Ones*

NATIVE AMERICAN
  Buffalo Dance
  Handgame Song*
  Mos' Mos'
  Round Dance

PHILIPPINES
  My Nipa Hut*
  Tinikling
  Planting Rice Is Never Fun*

POLYNESIA
  Welcome Song*

RUSSIA
  Little Bird*
  Minka
  Volga Boat Song

SCANDINAVIA
  Clapping Land

*Sung in native language.

Sources:

Phyllis Gelineau, *Songs in Action*, New York: McGraw Hill, 1974.

Patricia Hackett, *The Melody Book*, Englewood Cliffs, NJ: Prentice-Hall, Inc., 1983.

Advancing Skills:

★ Play *What State Am I?* using countries and continents rather than states. Several children may wish to body sculpt all countries which constitute one continent.

★ Give the children pictures of people from various nations. Ask the children to research the customs and living conditions of the country represented and to write an autobiography of the person on his or her picture. The child should then assume the characterization of the person in the picture and orally present his or her autobiography.

What Will You Do?

(Improvisation)

The following are role-playing improvisations. You might wish to allow several students to interpret each improvisation so that different options can be explored. Some teachers also like to play these once and then repeat them, asking the students to switch roles and to move the plot in a new direction.

Improvisations:

Who: You and a friend
What: You have hurt your friend's feelings. What will you do?

Who: You and your teacher
What: You forgot to do your homework. What will you do?

Who: You and a bully at school
What: You want the bully to stop bothering you. What will you do?

Who: You and a friend
What: You find money on the playground. What will you do?

Who: You and your classmate
What: Your classmate copies from you. What will you do?

Who: You and your best friend
What: You can't find your lunch money. What will you do?

Who: You and your parents
What: You want permission to go on a field trip but you have been grounded. What will you do?

Who: You and a new classmate
What: You want to be friends with him or her but your other friends don't like the new student. What will you do?

Radio Station T-R-I-P

(Characterization)

Children have surfed a variety of communication networks: television channels, computer networks, and radio stations. Communication depends upon both speaker and listener sharing meaning. Trying to make sense of sound bites when whole sentences are needed, as illustrated in the characterization activity which follows, sometimes results in noise on the network. Invite children to imagine rapidly changing radio stations. Cast three children who will use voice and rapid cue pickup to interpret the roles of the announcer, weather forecaster, and travel show host. When the radio is turned off, ask the listeners what meanings have been shared.

Announcer: Welcome to station T-R-I-P, located near the top of your dial. Today, you'll hear . . .

Weather Forecaster: . . . a tropical rainstorm. Further to the north, they'll be having . . .

Travel Show Host: . . . the cruise of a lifetime. You'll stop at exotic ports and see . . .

Weather Forecaster: . . . blizzard conditions. If you wear protective clothing, however, you'll . . .

Announcer: . . . take calls from our listeners who want to know . . .

Travel Show Host: . . . if you experience jet lag. To prevent this . . .

Announcer: . . . shop at the big Going Out of Business Sale today . . .

Weather Forecaster: . . . on the weather map. We predict . . .

Travel Show Host: . . . very little turbulence. Once you arrive at your destination city, you'll be met by one of our experienced guides who will . . .

Announcer: . . . be playing the hits for you again after this commercial message.

What's Our Line?

(Characterization)

Children should play this activity in small groups. Each group should research the characteristics of a reference source, such as the almanac, atlas, encyclopedia, dictionary, and glossary. As a group, they should create a series of clues, each beginning with, "I am . . ."

Example:

"I am in the library. I am filled with the correct spelling of words."

Each group then presents their clues orally to the other groups. Classmates identify the reference source based upon the clues.

Chapter 9

TECHNOLOGY

Content	Music/Creative Drama	
Tools of Technology	Noisy Story:	I Work in an Office
	Movement:	Hardware/Software
Movement of Technology	Sequence Game:	Processing Practices
	Quieting Activities:	Down Time
	Movement:	Technology Choreography
Sounds of Technology	Noisy Story:	The Computer Family
	Scavenger Hunt:	Work Sounds
	Improvisation:	Technology Talk
	Found Sound:	Inaudible Made Audible: Instruments for 2025
Futuristic Technology	Body Sculptures:	Suzy's Science Project
	Story Creation:	In the Future
		Technology Tales
Operations Technology	Story Creation:	Sandy the Saboteur

Technology fascinates children. They readily grasp the usefulness of modern tools to help us work. The following activities raise the children's awareness of technology's role and presence in their world.

I Work in an Office

(Noisy Story)

This noisy story is cleverly punctuated with the technological sounds of today's office.

Report — Read me, read me	*Telephone — Rrrrring*
Copy Machine — Crank 'em out, Crank 'em out	*Computer — Enter data, enter data*
Answering Machine — At the sound of the beep	*Fax — Quickly, quickly*

Welcome to my office where I work. First, let me turn on my computer*. Next, I'll turn off the telephone* answering machine* and plug in the coffee maker. My boss has left a report* for me to type on my computer*. I begin typing the report*, but the telephone* rings. I answer the telephone* and then finish the report* on the computer*. Now, I need to make copies of the report* on the copy machine*. While the copy machine* runs, I check the coffee maker. The coffee is done. The telephone* rings again. It is my boss. She wants me to pick up a fax* in another office and to fax* the report* I just typed on the computer*. I pick up the copies from the copy machine* and put all but one on my desk. Because I'm leaving my office, I turn on the telephone* answering machine*. I go to the office next door to pick up a fax* and to fax* the report*. Then, I come back to my office. I pour myself a cup of coffee and sit down at my computer*. I turn off the telephone* answering machine*. I need to get busy. I have a lot of letters and memos to type on my computer*.

Advancing Skill:

★ Use found sounds in conjunction with the story sounds associated with the machines.

Hardware/Software

(Movement)

This activity is designed to assist young children in contrasting the hardware and software used in computers. The children should walk clockwise in a circle. Whenever the teacher calls out the term "hardware," the children should walk stiffly with hands held in front of them. Whenever they hear the term "software," they should relax their bodies and walk limply, like rag dolls, around the circle. Once children appear adept at listening, the speed at which the terms are alternated can be increased.

Advancing Skill:

★ Add other calls to those of hardware and software. When the children hear "together," they should find a partner and link arms. One walks stiffly as hardware and the other limply as software. To resume walking individually, call "remove disk," an instruction for the "software child" to leave the other. Upon completing the exercise, the children can describe how their movements contrasted when they walked individually and how they moved when walking with a partner. Challenge third graders to describe an analogy to hardware and software working together in a computer.

Processing Practices

(Sequence Game)

Understanding how a computer processes information can sometimes be intimidating for young learners. The following sequence game illustrates the basic steps in information processing.

Before beginning the game, the teacher should tape four lines on the floor, using noon, three, six, and nine o'clock positions for locations. The line at the noon position should be labeled "On." Directly opposite, the line should be labeled "Off." The line at the three o'clock position should be labeled "In," and the nine o'clock line should be labeled "Out."

Distribute cards to the players, reminding them to watch carefully for their cues.

You start the game. Cross over the "On" line and come to the center of the room. Sit down at an imaginary keyboard and pantomime typing in data.

The person before you has crossed over the "On" line and come to the center of the room, sat down at an imaginary keyboard, and pantomimed typing in data.

You come to the center of the room by crossing over the "In" line. Hug yourself and say in a robot-like voice, "Holding data."

The person before you has come to the center of the room by crossing over the "In" line. He or she has hugged him or herself and said in a robot-like voice, "Holding data."

You come to the center of the room and move your hand to and from your heart three times and then point to your brain, saying, "Processing is the heart and mind of a computer."

The person before you has come to the center of the room, moved his or her hand to and from the heart three times, pointed to the brain, and said, "Processing is the heart and mind of a computer."

You come to the center of the room and pantomime putting boxes on a shelf. When you are finished, sit down, and say, "Store and wait."

The person before you has come to the center of the room and pantomimed putting boxes on a shelf, sat down, and said, "Store and wait."

You cross the "Out" line and come to the center of the room. Move your finger across an imaginary screen and say, "Checking video display unit." Cross over the "Out" line again and say, "Printing."

The person before you has crossed the "Out" line and come to the center of the room, moved his or her finger across an imaginary screen, and said, "Checking video display unit." He or she then crossed over the "Out" line again and said, "Printing."

You come to the center of the room. Pantomime lifting paper from a printer and reading. Cross over the "Out" line and say, "All done for now."

Down Time
(Quieting Activities)

Just as children get tired when their energy lags, mechanical devices can also slow down, as these quieting activities illustrate. Play them as you would those on page 237.

You are a battery-operated toy and your batteries run down until you stop.

You are a garage door and someone is raising and lowering you by using a garage door opener. First, rise up to let the car in and then lower yourself down slowly.

You are singing on a music video and the person watching pushes the pause button on the VCR.

Technology Choreography

(Movement)

Though "high tech(nology)" rarely has been accused of being "high touch" or emotive in nature, students can learn about technology and interpret their understandings through creative movement.

Begin by providing a prepared tape recording (no more than three minutes) of the sounds of various machines, such as an electric can opener, microwave, coffee maker, or mixer. It is not necessary to have many sounds. Rather, juxtapose the sounds of different lengths and repeat them during the three-minute recording.

After the students identify the source of the sounds, discuss the ways in which technology (in the kitchen, sewing room, garage, or other places) helps us do our work. Assign students to work in pairs or alone to prepare a choreographed interpretation of the sounds on the tape. Ask the children to think about the function of the technology as they select movements. Play the tape three or four times for rehearsal and preparation. Encourage students to select appropriate movement, depending upon the function and "feeling" of the technology. The interpretation may take the form of finger movements, a hand jive, dance, or creative movement. Perform the choreographs and critique the movements as to their connection with the function of technology.

The Computer Family

(Noisy Story)

While most children today are familiar with computers, not all may realize that the machines vary in size and capability. The following noisy story illustrates this point.

Daddy Mainframe Computer — I'm the biggest   *Data — Things given*
Mommy Minicomputer — I'm the middle size   *Memory — Don't forget!*
Baby Microcomputer — I'm the smallest

The Computer family, Daddy Mainframe Computer*, Mommy Minicomputer*, and Baby Microcomputer* are eager to start their day.

Daddy Mainframe Computer* works in a scientific laboratory helping to build satellites. Daddy Mainframe Computer* can process a lot of data*. "I have a large memory*," Daddy Mainframe Computer* likes to boast. "I store important data*."

Mommy Minicomputer* works in a hospital. Mommy Minicomputer* is proud of the help she gives doctors and nurses. "I use data* to make people feel better," Mommy Minicomputer* says with delight.

"Oh, my," thinks Baby Microcomputer*. "Daddy Mainframe Computer* and Mommy Minicomputer*, you do such important jobs. My memory* is too small. I'll never be like you. I can only store a little data*." Baby Microcomputer* feels so sad and embarrassed that he is certain that his keyboard will freeze.

"Come now, Baby Microcomputer*," says Mommy Minicomputer* tenderly, "you do many important jobs. It is you, Baby Microcomputer*, that people take with them as laptops. You see many places."

"You may not have as much memory* as I do," says Daddy Mainframe Computer*, "but you help people to do their work no matter where they are."

"I sit on top of a desk all day," adds Mommy Minicomputer*, "and Daddy Mainframe Computer* takes up an entire room. We cannot travel. You, Baby Microcomputer*, can store data* anywhere. You will see the world."

Baby Microcomputer* beams. "My memory* stores important data*," he thinks. "I may be small, but I am powerful," Baby Microcomputer* tell his parents. Daddy Mainframe Computer* and Mommy Minicomputer* smile proudly at their child.

Work Sounds

(Scavenger Hunt)

Much of the technology that is used in offices, hospitals, and other work environments has characteristic sounds. Even a trip to the grocery store will unveil machines that weigh items electronically, scanners that record bar codes and item prices, scanning "guns" that check shelf pricing, store doors that electronically coach you to walk faster/slower as they revolve, and so on.

To help children become familiar with technology in the working environment, assign them to tape record a number of sounds made by equipment in various workplaces. For example, the next time a child goes to the dentist, he or she can record a variety of sounds from that environment. The sounds of that workplace can be shared and discussed when the tape is played for the entire class.

Technology Talk
(Improvisation)

This activity encourages students to imitate and manipulate the sounds of technology to form an original composition. Begin by asking students to make an inventory list of any type of technology (tools, appliances, or machines) they know. Next to the particular technology, ask the students to imitate and write the sounds which the machine makes. For example, the inventory might begin with the many sounds of a computer, fax machine, telephone, or doorbell:

TECHNOLOGY	*SOUND*
Computer	Click (as the machine is switched on) Shirr (as it starts up) Beep (as the operating system begins) Hum (while the machine works)
Fax Machine	Clack (to signal an incoming message) Buzz (as paper flows through) Bleep (to signal the message is finished) Clack (to turn off the printer)
Telephone	Ring (for an incoming call) Bip (for the busy signal) Hee Haw (when the phone is off the hook) Tone (to signal it is working to dial) Different pitches (when touch tone registers different numbers)

Doorbell	Chime
	Ring
	Buzz
	Clang
	Ding Dong

Discuss how the technology sounds have different lengths, volume, and pitches. Group the children into teams of three or four. Ask them to select one of the forms of technology and improvise a one-minute composition using the sounds. The audience members should listen and try to imagine the machine's function during the improvisation.

Discuss with the students reasons why certain technology sounds might be high/low, loud/soft, short/long, or intermittent/regular.

Inaudible Made Audible: Instruments for 2025
(Found Sound)

Remind the children that technology has helped our senses become more acute in detecting sounds, visuals, textures, temperatures, fragrances, and so forth. To illustrate, discuss how the microscope and an x-ray machine help us see things that the ordinary eye cannot.

Current technology also expands the repertory of our senses with images made by computers or musical sounds made by synthesizers. What can we imagine for the future of instruments? One day we may be able to "hear" and imitate the sounds of events happening on a micro-level. For example, acousticians are now recording the sounds of atoms bumping into one another in molecules.

Ask the children to think about events that are happening at currently inaudible levels, such as leaves sprouting on trees, mercury rising in a thermometer, rocks eroding, clouds traveling, iron oxidizing, and cells dividing. Using found sounds, assign children to create a sound piece (one minute long) to depict these events.

Discuss what type of technology might be needed to record currently inaudible sounds. How might these instruments of 2025 help us do our work?

Suzy's Science Project

(Body Sculptures)

Science projects and school science fairs give children hands-on opportunities to examine, test, and operate technical devices. These experiences can be applied to the more fanciful invention in the following activity.

Children working in small groups create Suzy's new invention using their bodies and machine-like sounds after hearing the following scenario. They may adapt a device currently in use, such as a computer, or create a futuristic contraption with a real or fantastic purpose.

> Suzy is a second grader in the year 2020. She has been assigned the creation of a new technological device as her science project. As a group, you are to become Suzy's invention. Your task is to create the device, name it, show how it works, and tell the rest of the class what it does.

In the Future

(Story Creation)

No idea is impossible as children envision the future while developing this story. The opening is shared orally with the class. With children seated in a circle, each adds as much or as little to the story as he or she likes. The last child adds a conclusion.

> "Good morning, Hal," John says to the television set as he walks into the room. "Good morning," says the television as Hal turns himself on for the day, "would you like to watch the news?"
>
> Hal is one of many automated devices that make life easy in the twenty-second century. Today, John is working on his latest invention. He . . .

Technology Tales

(Story Creation)

Divide the children into groups and give each group a paper bag containing slips of paper with the name of an electronic invention written on each one. The following devices are suggested.

> Microwave oven
> Computer
> Radar
> Radio
> Tape recorder
> Compact disk player
> Videocassette recorder
> X-ray machine
> Calculator

A child begins a story, another continues it, and so on until all have participated. For this exercise, however, before the child contributes, he or she takes a slip of paper from the bag and must find a way to work the invention into the story. Children need only draw one slip and they may have more than one turn. (This is especially useful if children have difficulty generating an idea and cannot find a way to incorporate the item until a second or third turn.) Before the story reaches a conclusion, all children should have had input and all electronic devices should be incorporated.

Sandy the Saboteur

(Story Creation)

This story creation activity relies on the importance of developing complications and resolutions and is most appropriate for advanced players. For best results, lead the activity following these steps.

1. Assign all of the children the task of researching how automated teller machines, robots, and video games work.

2. Ask the children to count off by twos. Then, divide into groups of number ones and number twos.

3. Ask the children to brainstorm ideas as to how these technological tools might be broken as well as how they might be fixed. After the brainstorming session, ask them to write a list of their best ideas on the board.

4. Seat the children in a circle, alternating ones (#1) and twos (#2).

5. Share with them the open-ended story starter that follows. Then, ask the children to continue the story using a good news/bad news format. A #1, for example, might offer a contribution that facilitates fixing the machine while a #2 would add something that prevents it from working. The next person then would have to address that complication. The last person should successfully resolve the problem. Be certain that the children know that their research should be included in their story contributions.

Sandy the Saboteur

"Ladies and gentlemen," the mayor said, "we have a problem in our fair city. Sandy the Saboteur has made all of the automated teller machines in our banks, robots in our automobile factories, and video games in our arcades stop working. Your task is to figure out how Sandy did it and to repair the damage. Good luck!" Looking around the room, I knew that the members of our group were all important scientists and detectives. First, we had to think about how . . .

Advancing Skill:

★ Divide the children into groups and, using the same beginning, have them create and dramatize a complete story about *Sandy the Saboteur*.

Chapter 10

MULTICULTURAL EDUCATION

Content	Music/Creative Drama	
Multicultural Awareness	Name Game:	Food and Country
		Favorite Foods
	Concentration Game:	Ethnic Food Fair
	Pantomime:	Italian Food
	Body Sculpture:	Country Cuisine
	Song:	The Tortillas Vendor
	Accompaniment:	Ethnic Instruments
	Song:	Oranges and Lemons
	Sequence Game:	Favorite Recipe
	Story Dramatization:	Folk Tales Around the World
	Orchestration:	The Dancing Lion
	Storytelling:	Waltzing Matilda

$\mathcal{M}$*usic and creative drama can serve as the connective tissue for multicultural content. Children can learn to appreciate diverse customs through the following activities. Integrate all areas of the curriculum—maps, foreign currencies, foreign languages—to extend the children's horizons.*

Food and Country

(Name Game)

As an introduction to multicultural studies, few things are as tempting as foods. Ethnic cuisine fuels the body and the mind as children name a native food they like and the country of origin in this name game.

My name is Carl and I like chop suey. Chop suey is from China.

My name is Ian and I like spaghetti. Spaghetti is from Italy.

Favorite Foods

(Name Game)

This is another name game that centers on ethnic foods. To play, each student says his or her first or last name and a favorite ethnic food that begins with the same first letter.

Example:

My first name is Michelle and I like matzo.
My last name is Kirk and I like kielbasa.

Ethnic Food Fair

(Concentration Game)

This activity presents an appetizing challenge. Each child repeats the starting phrase and the foods already named before adding one item to the list. As a special treat, the boys and girls might consider having a real ethnic food fair in the classroom.

Teacher: We are having a food fair at school. We are going to eat gyros.

Child 1:   We are having a food fair at school. We are going to eat gyros and baklava.

Child 2:   We are having a food fair at school. We are going to eat gyros, baklava, and moussaka.

Advancing Skill:

★ Invite members of the community to teach the children how to make their favorite ethnic recipes.

Italian Food

(Pantomime)

The following pantomime can assist children in further connecting ethnic foods to their country of origin. Before playing this activity, ask the students to locate Italy on a map or globe. Suggest that they do library research or visit local Italian restaurants to find out what other foods are associated with this country. This activity can be adapted for other ethnic foods and their countries of origin.

You are cutting a pizza pie, taking a slice of pizza, and eating it.

You are twirling spaghetti onto your fork and then taking a big bite.

You are preparing lasagna by alternating layers of meat, cheese, sauce, and noodles in a baking pan and then putting the pan in the oven.

You are kneading dough and then shaping it into a loaf of Italian bread.

You are eating cold spumoni and your teeth are chattering.

Country Cuisine
(Body Sculpture)

In groups, form the geographic outlines of countries named in the previous exercise.

Advancing Skill:

★ Invite the children to learn a folk dance from one of the countries outlined through body sculpture. Identify fundamental movements in the dance.

The Tortillas Vendor
(Song)

This beautiful love song from Chile concerns a vendor selling tortillas in the evening. The vendor strolls down the street of his girlfriend, singing loudly for her to come out and buy tostadas and tortillas.

No-cheos-cu-ra, na-da ve-o, Pe-ro lle-vo mi fa-rol, — — Por tus puer-tas, voy pa-san-do, Y can-tan-do con a-mor.___ Mas___ voy can-tan-do___ Con___ har-ta pe-na,___ Quien com-pra mis___ tos-ta-di-tas,___ Tor-ti-llas bue-nas.

Refrain:

Advancing Skills:

★ Feel the song moving in a triple meter (three beats per measure pattern). Invite the children to create a simple stroll that fits the movement of the song.

★ Ask the children to find out what ingredients are required for tortillas. Why would these foods be popular in Chile? What foods are grown in Chile? How is food prepared?

★ Extend the research to other items made in Chile or South America.

Ethnic Instruments

(Accompaniment)

Some classroom instruments are closely connected with ethnic music. For example, maracas are often used in Hispanic and Mexican music. Drums play a big role in many different cultures. Students may research the history of instruments to incorporate them into the accompaniment of songs.

Oranges and Lemons
(Song)

Sing the following song without revealing the song's ethnic origin. Ask the children to listen a second time for one clue ("farthings") which might help them identify the source.

Advancing Skills:

★ Inspire the children to research what a farthing is worth.

★ As a group, create new verses using different foods, currency denominations, and locations of various cultures, *e.g.*, substitute rice and beans for foods, pesos for currency, and Juarez for St. Clements.

Favorite Recipe

(Sequence Game)

In preparation for this activity, ask the children to select an ethnic food and to find a recipe for making it. The necessary steps for food preparation will have to be identified and written on cards in sequence game form. Each step is described in action terms on the cards.

Example:

Hamantaschen*

> You start the game. Come to the center of the room and pantomime measuring and mixing 2½ cups all-purpose flour, ½ cup sugar, and 1 teaspoon baking powder in a large bowl.

> The person before you has pantomimed measuring and mixing 2½ cups all-purpose flour, ½ cup sugar, and 1 teaspoon baking powder in a large bowl.
>
> *You come to the center of the room and pantomime adding ¾ cup (1½ sticks) of margarine or butter to the bowl. Cut in margarine with pastry blender until mixture resembles fine crumbs.*

> The person before you has come to the center of the room and pantomimed adding ¾ cup (1½ sticks) of margarine or butter to the bowl and cutting in margarine with pastry blender until the mixture resembles fine crumbs.
>
> *You come to the center of the room and pantomime mixing 1 teaspoon lemon peel, ½ teaspoon vanilla, and 2 eggs into the flour mixture.*

The person before you has come to the center of the room and pantomimed mixing 1 teaspoon lemon peel, ½ teaspoon vanilla, and 2 eggs into the flour mixture.

You come to the center of the room and pantomime kneading the mixture into a dough ball. Pantomime adding ¼ cup flour if the dough is too sticky to handle.

The person before you has come to the center of the room and pantomimed kneading the mixture into a dough ball and adding ¼ cup flour if the dough is too sticky to handle.

You come to the center of the room and pantomime covering the bowl and putting it in the refrigerator for two hours or until the mixture is firm.

The person before you has come to the center of the room and pantomimed covering a bowl and putting it in the refrigerator for two hours or until the mixture is firm.

You come to the center of the room and pantomime heating the oven to 350 degrees. Remove the bowl from the refrigerator.

The person before you has come to the center of the room and pantomimed heating the oven to 350 degrees and removing the bowl from the refrigerator.

You come to the center of the room and pantomime lightly flouring and covering a board with cloth, rolling half the dough at a time onto the board, and flattening the dough into a ⅛ inch thickness as you roll it.

The person before you has come to the center of the room and pantomimed lightly flouring and covering a board with cloth, rolling half the dough at a time onto the board, and flattening the dough into a ⅛ inch thickness as he or she rolled it.

You come to the center of the room and pantomime cutting the dough into three-inch rounds.

The person before you has come to the center of the room and pantomimed cutting the dough into three-inch rounds.

You come to the center of the room and pantomime spooning a level teaspoon of apricot, plum, or poppyseed filling onto each round.

The person before you has come to the center of the room and pantomimed spooning a level teaspoon of apricot, plum, or poppyseed filling onto each round.

You come to the center of the room and pantomime bringing up three sides of the round, using a metal spatula to form a triangle around the filling, and pinching the edges together.

The person before you has come to the center of the room and pantomimed bringing up three sides of the round, using a metal spatula to form a triangle around the filling and pinching the edges together.

You come to the center of the room and pantomime placing the rounds two inches apart on an ungreased cookie sheet, putting the sheet in the oven, and baking the rounds for 12–15 minutes.

The person before you has come to the center of the room and pantomimed placing the rounds two inches apart on an ungreased cookie sheet, putting the sheet in the oven, and baking the rounds for 12–15 minutes.

You come to the center of the room and pantomime removing the hamantaschen from the oven, taking them off the cookie sheet, and placing them on a wire rack to cool.

The person before you has come to the center of the room and pantomimed removing the hamantaschen from the oven, taking them off the cookie sheet, and placing them on a wire rack to cool.

You come to the center of the room and pantomime eating your cookies.

*Hamantaschen are cookies traditionally associated with the Jewish holiday of Purim. They are reminders of how the early Persian prime minister, Haman, was thwarted in his efforts to destroy the Jews.

Folk Tales Around the World

(Story Dramatization)

Our students are always surprised to learn that similar versions of favorite tales appear in many different parts of the world. Young students will experience a similarly delightful revelation when they dramatize different versions of a story as told in several countries. For example, **Cinderella** can be found in various versions and lends itself well to this activity. When students select a tale and find various versions through reading and research, the educational advantages are even more striking.

The Dancing Lion
(Orchestration)

A story may be orchestrated using song, band, and dancing to enhance its meaning. This story uses the talents of actors, singers, instrumentalists, and dancers. Read the children the following folktale, telling them it is from Africa.

Once upon a time, a man and woman lived in a very beautiful village in the valley. This village was full of people who loved music. They sang and danced and played instruments often. They were a happy people. But the woman was lonely for her mother and father. She hadn't seen them in a long time. So she told her husband that she wanted to go visit them for a few days. The man said, "Okay, but be very careful. There are mountain lions, and it is very dangerous when you cross the pass." "I'll be careful," she said, and packed her things. She began her journey to her mother's and father's village.

After three days, the man began to worry because the woman had not returned. So he set out to look for her. He packed a small bag and, because he was a musician, he brought an instrument with him. He didn't get very far when, all of a sudden, he saw a huge mountain lion looking very mean and hungry. The lion was walking toward the man. Just then, a rabbit popped out of a bunny hole. The rabbit froze still when he saw the lion, hoping the lion did not see him.

The rabbit saw that the man had an instrument in his backpack, so he whispered, "Give me the instrument. I have an idea." The man tossed him the instrument as the lion drew near. The rabbit began playing the instrument: ♪♫♪♫♪

The lion loved the music and was distracted by it. He began dancing to the music. He was having a good old time. And this went on for quite a while. The rabbit, however, became tired and stopped playing. The lion stopped dancing at once and was even more angry. He liked the music. It made him forget how hungry he was. He looked around and growled.

The scared rabbit began playing again. The lion began dancing immediately. The rabbit said to the man, "You better move on while the lion is so busy dancing. He will never notice you." So, the man began running home while the music was louder and the lion danced more happily.

Meanwhile, the rabbit began moving closer and closer to his bunny hole, while he played the instrument faster and faster: ♪♫♪♫♪

The lion danced faster and faster to the music: ♪♫♪♫♪

All of a sudden, the rabbit jumped into the hole and the music stopped.

The lion stopped. He looked to the left. He looked to the right. He couldn't imagine what happened to the music. He frowned because he was having such a good time and the music stopped. He looked to the left again. He looked to the right. He looked all around. Finally, he stomped away, sad that the fun was over.

The folktale has many opportunities to integrate pantomime, rhythm instruments, singing, dancing, masks, and language arts. Cast the parts of the man, woman, mountain lion, and rabbit. The remainder of the children can be villagers who sing for the introduction and the coda (finale) and dance at the outset of the tale. One child needs to play an instrument (of his or her choice) at the "♪♫♪♫♪" symbols. (The teacher may merely gesture to the child at the performance points.)

As an art project, have the children make headdresses or masks for a character of their choice. See the illustrations below for simple art projects using paper bags.

Teach the children the following song and rhythm band piece. It is based upon the rhythms of **Che Che Koolay**, an African chant. It can be used at the introduction of the performance, when describing the musical village, and at the conclusion of the tale. Notice the song is in "call and response" form. A leader sings the line and the chorus repeats it:

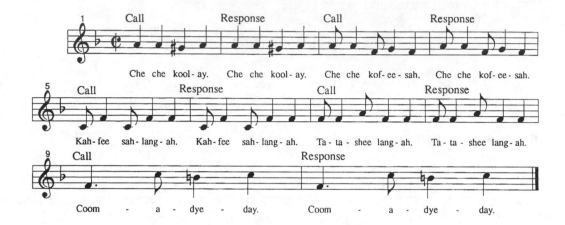

Koolay Band

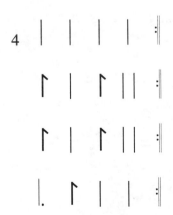

Be generous in allowing sufficient preparation time for the chorus, band, and players. Give the child who serves as the rabbit ample time to plan how he or she will play the instrument at the designated "♪♫♪♫♪" sections. Allow time for the rabbit and lion to coordinate some of their improvised movements.

Waltzing Matilda

(Storytelling)

The poems and songs of other countries enliven the study of literature and geography. *Waltzing Matilda* is a well-known Australian poem that has been popularized in song. Children should be encouraged to locate Australia on a map or globe. As a part of a language arts lesson, young people can be challenged to find the meaning of the terms which are strange to Americans but understood by Australians. (The words are explained in the retelling which follows.) Use the synopsis or the poem in its entirety as the basis for a story dramatization. Spend time developing characterizations. An exploration of Australian history will enrich play by enabling the children to better understand who the swagman, the squatter, and the policemen might be.

Waltzing Matilda

Oh there once was a swagman camped in the billabongs,
    Under the shade of a Coolibah tree;
And he sang as he looked at the old billy boiling,
    "Who'll come a-waltzing Matilda with me."

"Who'll come a-waltzing Matilda, my darling,
    Who'll come a-waltzing Matilda with me.
Waltzing Matilda and leading a water-bag,
    Who'll come a-waltzing Matilda with me."

Up came the jumbuck to drink at the waterhole,
    Up jumped the swagman and he grabbed him in glee;
And he sang as he put him away in his tucker-bag,
    "You'll come a-waltzing Matilda with me."

"Who'll come a-waltzing Matilda, my darling,
    Who'll come a-waltzing Matilda with me.
Waltzing Matilda and leading a water-bag,
    Who'll come a-waltzing Matilda with me."

Up came a squatter a-riding his thoroughbred;
    Up came policemen — one, two, and three.
"Whose is the jumbuck you've got in your tucker-bag?
    You'll come a-waltzing Matilda with we."

"Who'll come a-waltzing Matilda, my darling,
    Who'll come a-waltzing Matilda with me.
Waltzing Matilda and leading a water-bag,
    Who'll come a-waltzing Matilda with me."

Up sprang the swagman and jumped in the waterhole,
    Drowning himself by the Coolibah tree;
And his voice can be heard as it sings in the billabongs,
    "Who'll come a-waltzing Matilda with me."

"Who'll come a-waltzing Matilda, my darling,
    Who'll come a-waltzing Matilda with me.
Waltzing Matilda and leading a water-bag,
    Who'll come a-waltzing Matilda with me."

"*Waltzing Matilda*," found in **A.B. "Banjo" Patterson's Collected Verse**, illustrations by Norman Lindsay, Hal Gye, and Lionel Lindsay. North Ryde, New South Wales, Australia: Angus & Robertson Publishers, 1986, 2nd ed., p. 194.

A swagman (drifter) was camped beside billabongs (water holes), waiting for his billy (tea) to boil, when a large jumbuck (sheep) appeared. The swagman captured the sheep and put it in his tucker bag (food bag). The squatter (landowner) appeared, as did three policemen, and tried to arrest the swagman. Rather than be captured, the swagman jumped into the pond and drowned. His voice can still be heard across the land.

Advancing Skills:

★ Encourage the children to create "The Adventures of the Swagman." Here, the children develop episodes which reveal the life of the swagman before that fateful day at the billabongs. Children will also enjoy learning and singing the poem in song form.

★ Make a sequence game from the poem. The children can dramatize the events in the story through the sequencing exercise.

★ Group the students and have each group research one of the following topics: 1) settling Australia; 2) life on an Australian sheep ranch; 3) living in the outback; and 4) Aboriginal culture. Ask them to create orally or in writing a story about the topic they have selected. They should then use the story as the basis for a story dramatization. They might also enjoy exchanging stories and dramatizing one that another group has generated.

Index